D0794073

JOHN
LEWIS

The African-American Biographies Series

MARIAN ANDERSON
Singer and Humanitarian
0-7660-1211-5

MAYA ANGELOU
More Than a Poet
0-89490-684-4

LOUIS ARMSTRONG
King of Jazz
0-89490-997-5

ARTHUR ASHE
Breaking the Color Barrier
in Tennis
0-89490-689-5

BENJAMIN BANNEKER
Astronomer and Mathematician
0-7660-1208-5

JULIAN BOND
Civil Rights Activist and Chairman of
the NAACP
0-7660-1549-1

RALPH BUNCHE
Winner of the Nobel Peace Prize
0-7660-1203-4

**GEORGE WASHINGTON
CARVER**
Scientist and Inventor
0-7660-1770-2

BESSIE COLEMAN
First Black Woman Pilot
0-7660-1545-9

FREDERICK DOUGLASS
Speaking Out Against Slavery
0-7660-1773-7

W. E. B. DU BOIS
Champion of Civil Rights
0-7660-1209-3

**PAUL LAURENCE
DUNBAR**
Portrait of a Poet
0-7660-1350-2

DUKE ELLINGTON
Giant of Jazz
0-89490-691-7

ARETHA FRANKLIN
Motown Superstar
0-89490-686-0

NIKKI GIOVANNI
Poet of the People
0-7660-1238-7

WHOOPI GOLDBERG
Comedian and Movie Star
0-7660-1205-0

FANNIE LOU HAMER
Fighting for the Right to Vote
0-7660-1772-9

LORRAINE HANSBERRY
Playwright and Voice of Justice
0-89490-945-2

MATTHEW HENSON
Co-Discoverer of the North Pole
0-7660-1546-7

LANGSTON HUGHES
Poet of the Harlem Renaissance
0-89490-815-4

ZORA NEALE HURSTON
Southern Storyteller
0-89490-685-2

JESSE JACKSON
Civil Rights Activist
0-7660-1390-1

QUINCY JONES
Musician, Composer, Producer
0-89490-814-6

BARBARA JORDAN
Congresswoman, Lawyer,
Educator
0-89490-692-5

CORETTA SCOTT KING
Striving for Civil Rights
0-89490-811-1

**MARTIN LUTHER
KING, JR.**
Leader for Civil Rights
0-89490-687-9

JOHN LEWIS
From Freedom Rider to Congressman
0-7660-1768-0

THURGOOD MARSHALL
Civil Rights Attorney and
Supreme Court Justice
0-7660-1547-5

KWEISI MFUME
Congressman and NAACP Leader
0-7660-1237-9

TONI MORRISON
Nobel Prize-Winning Author
0-89490-688-7

WALTER DEAN MYERS
Writer for Real Teens
0-7660-1206-9

JESSE OWENS
Track and Field Legend
0-89490-812-X

COLIN POWELL
Soldier and Patriot
0-89490-810-3

A. PHILIP RANDOLPH
Union Leader and Civil Rights
Crusader
0-7660-1544-0

PAUL ROBESON
Actor, Singer, Political Activist
0-89490-944-4

JACKIE ROBINSON
Baseball's Civil Rights Legend
0-89490-690-9

BETTY SHABAZZ
Sharing the Vision
of Malcolm X
0-7660-1210-7

HARRIET TUBMAN
Moses of the Underground Railroad
0-7660-1548-3

MADAM C. J. WALKER
Self-Made Businesswoman
0-7660-1204-2

IDA B. WELLS-BARNETT
Crusader Against Lynching
0-89490-947-9

OPRAH WINFREY
Talk Show Legend
0-7660-1207-7

CARTER G. WOODSON
Father of African-American History
0-89490-946-0

RICHARD WRIGHT
Author of *Native Son* and *Black Boy*
0-7660-1769-9

—African-American Biographies—

JOHN LEWIS

From Freedom Rider to Congressman

Series Consultant:
Dr. Russell L. Adams, Chairman
Department of Afro-American Studies, Howard University

Christine M. Hill

Enslow Publishers, Inc.

40 Industrial Road   PO Box 38
Box 398   Aldershot
Berkeley Heights, NJ 07922 Hants GU12 6BP
USA   UK

http://www.enslow.com

Library of Congress Cataloging-in-Publication Data

Hill, Christine M.
　　John Lewis : from freedom rider to Congressman / Christine M. Hill.
　　　　p. cm. — (African-American biographies)
　　Includes bibliographical references and index.
　　Summary: Chronicles the life of the man whose politics took him from
civil rights worker in the South to serving as a United States Congressman.
　　ISBN 0-7660-1768-0 (hardcover)
　　1. Lewis, John, 1940 Feb. 21—Juvenile literature. 2. Legislators—United
States—Biography—Juvenile literature. 3. African American legislators—
Biography—Juvenile literature. 4. United States. Congress. House—
Biography—Juvenile literature. 5. African American civil rights workers—
Biography—Juvenile literature. 6. African Americans—Civil rights—
Southern States—History—20th century—Juvenile literature. 7. Civil
rights movements—Southern States—History—20th century—Juvenile
literature. 8. Lewis, John, 1940 Feb. 21– [1. Civil rights workers.
2. Legislators. 3. African Americans—Biography.] I. Title. II. Series.
E840.8.L43 H55　2002
323.1'196073'0092—dc21
　　　　　　　　　　　　　　　　　　　　　2001006718

Printed in the United States of America

10 9 8 7 6 5 4 3 2 1

To Our Readers:
We have done our best to make sure all Internet Addresses in this book were active
and appropriate when we went to press. However, the author and the publisher
have no control over and assume no liability for the material available on those
Internet sites or on other Web sites they may link to. Any comments or suggestions
can be sent by e-mail to comments@enslow.com or to the address on the back
cover.

Every effort has been made to locate all copyright holders of material used in this
book. If any errors or omissions have occurred, corrections will be made in future
editions of this book.

Illustration Credits: Associated Press, p. 39; Courtesy of the Atlanta
History Center, p. 97; Library of Congress, p. 14, 77, 80; Library of
Congress, Prints & Photographs Division, U.S. News & World Report
Magazine Collection, pp. 25, 35, 44, 48, 58, 64, 68, 73, 84, 90;
Morehouse College, Office of Alumni Relations, Atlanta, Georgia, p. 101;
Photo courtesy of Congressman John Lewis, pp. 10, 16, 31, 110.

Cover Illustration: Photo courtesy of Congressman John Lewis

Contents

Acknowledgment

The author wishes to thank
Congressman John Lewis
for reading the manuscript.

1

FREEDOM RIDER

Greyhound bus pulled into the terminal at Rock Hill, South Carolina, on May 9, 1961. John Lewis, a black man, and Albert Bigelow, a white man, sat side by side in front seats. By sitting together on the bus, they were breaking a state law. As they rose to enter the terminal, they planned to break the state law again. They were Freedom Riders.

Lewis headed for one of the two waiting rooms, the one with the sign reading "WHITE." Bigelow headed for the room labeled "COLORED." Two white teenagers lounged at the entrance to the white waiting room. Cigarettes dangled from their lips as they combed their ducktail haircuts. They stared at Lewis. One of them blocked his path, snarling a racial insult.

"I have a right to go in here." Lewis spoke calmly and quietly.[1]

Lewis felt the thud of a fist on the side of his head. A second blow smashed into his face. He staggered and fell. His ribs stung from vicious kicks. He tasted his own blood but he did not resist. They were "going into the valley of the shadow of death," he thought.[2] All this time, a police officer had been observing the scene. Finally, he called off the attackers and sent them home. Lewis refused to press charges.

A month before, Lewis had been attending college at the American Baptist Theological Seminary in Nashville, Tennessee. A friend showed him a magazine advertisement for the Congress of Racial Equality (CORE). The organization was seeking volunteers to challenge segregation on interstate buses. The test would be called the Freedom Ride. Lewis had already been active for several years in the civil rights movement in Nashville. This was just the opportunity he had been waiting for: It was a chance to confront an issue of national importance.

The laws of most southern states in 1961 required all the black passengers and white passengers to sit separately on buses—whites in the front, blacks in the back. Bus terminals had two sets of waiting rooms, restaurants, and rest rooms. Even drinking fountains were marked "WHITE" and "COLORED." But the previous year, the United States Supreme Court had ruled that when a bus route crossed state lines, it was no longer subject to local laws. Instead it was subject to federal laws. State laws segregating passengers whose journeys crossed state lines were unconstitutional. Interstate passengers could sit anywhere they liked, and they could use any station facilities. However, southern states defied the Supreme Court ruling and continued to enforce local laws. CORE intended to confront their refusal to obey the Court's decision.

CORE chose thirteen volunteers, seven white and six black. John Lewis, at twenty-one, was one of the youngest. He had written on his application that he was willing "to give up all if necessary for the Freedom Ride, that Justice and Freedom might come to the Deep South."[3]

Lewis went to Washington, D.C., for training in nonviolent resistance. The volunteers practiced responding calmly to jeers and abuse. They resolved to go limp when attacked. Their journey would take them from Washington, D.C., to New Orleans, Louisiana, through eight segregated states.

On the night before the trip started, John Lewis dined out for the first time. Growing up in Alabama

John Lewis was ready to risk his life for justice and freedom.

and going to school in Nashville, he had never eaten in an elegant restaurant. He had never sat with blacks and whites together, conversing pleasantly over dinner. He savored the unfamiliar, but delicious, Chinese food. He admired the handsome, silvery serving platters. But none of the volunteers could forget the next day's purpose. "It was like the Last Supper," Lewis said, "because you didn't know what to expect, going on the Freedom Ride."[4]

The first stop the next day was Fredericksburg, Virginia. The Freedom Riders noticed that the "WHITE ONLY" and "COLORED ONLY" signs had been removed from the bus station. The next stops in Virginia were Richmond and Petersburg. Hostile stares greeted them, but nothing else. In Farmville, Virginia, the offensive signs still hung, newly painted. The Freedom Riders used the rest rooms and snack bar unchallenged, though. After two more small Virginia towns, the bus stopped in Charlotte, North Carolina. A black Freedom Rider was arrested for trespassing when he tried to get a shoeshine at a whites-only stand in Charlotte.

In North Carolina, Lewis sat on the bus with Hank Thomas, a Howard University student. Thomas realized that Lewis had accepted a greater purpose for his life. Lewis had spoken with perfect calm, Thomas later remembered, of being ready to die on the trip. If Lewis accepted the possibility of death, then he would be unafraid to do whatever was necessary to win equal rights for all Americans.[5]

Lewis's determination and his courage—which would one day carry him to the halls of the United States Congress—grew out of years of poverty, struggle, and the realization that social inequality would continue until people like him stood up and fought against it.

2

SHARECROPPERS' SON

John Robert Lewis was born on February 21, 1940, in rural Dunn's Chapel, Alabama. He was the third of ten children born to Eddie and Willie Mae Lewis. His parents were sharecroppers, farming some land that belonged to a wealthy white landowner. Sharecropping meant that any profits from the sale of crops would be divided between the owner and the tenant farmer. The same landowner also rented property to Mrs. Lewis's father, brother, and other relatives.

By the time John was four years old, his parents had saved $300 to buy a 110-acre farm of their own.

Though they now worked their own land, the family's income did not increase much. The Lewises raised corn, peanuts, okra, and other crops to sell, as well as food for their own table. In addition to their farm work, Mrs. Lewis did laundry and cleaning for white families and Mr. Lewis drove a school bus. The children worked on the family farm and in other farmers' fields, particularly in cotton season, "to get money for books or clothing for school," Lewis remembered.[1]

These sharecropper's children in Pike County, Alabama, take a ride in their new wagon in 1939. John, too, was born into a Pike County sharecropper's family around that time.

Young John, whose family called him by his middle name, Robert, hated farm chores. "I was always a complaining child," he admitted.[2] His family was relieved when he found a chore he liked—raising chickens. "I fell in love with them," Lewis said. "I named them, talked to them, assigned them to coops and guided them in every night and when one of them died, I preached his funeral and buried him. I also protested when one of them was killed for food. I refused to eat. I guess that was my first protest demonstration."[3]

The area of Alabama where John grew up was very poor. None of his neighbors had electricity or indoor plumbing until the 1950s, when John was in his teens. The county government did not bother to pave roads in places where only African Americans lived. The county had two separate school systems, one for blacks and one for whites. John's elementary school was a two-room wooden shack.

Despite the run-down building, John loved school from the very first day. He particularly loved reading, and he devoured biographies and true stories about the world beyond Alabama. Reading opened his mind to the possibility of a different kind of life.

When John was eleven years old, his uncle Otis, principal of a black school in another Alabama town, arranged for him to spend the summer with relatives in Buffalo, New York. Seeing blacks and whites shopping, traveling, and eating together, even living side by side, came as a revelation to John. "Home would never feel the same as it did before that trip," he said later. "The signs of segregation that had perplexed me up till then now outright angered me."[4]

Dunn's Chapel Elementary School ended with sixth grade. John attended the local junior high school in grades seven to nine and then went to Pike County Training School. There was no true high school for African-American students in the county. The training school was intended to teach African-American boys to be farmers or laborers and prepared the girls to be maids or housewives. A few outstanding students might go on to teacher training. John rode to school on a ramshackle bus that constantly broke down. On rainy days, it often skidded off the unpaved red clay roads. When this happened, the students were expected to get out and push it back onto the road.

From the start, John loved school, especially reading. He posed for this school portrait when he was eleven years old.

At harvest time, the Lewis children, like many farm children, stayed home from school to bring in the crops. John tried to hide under the house and make a break for the school bus when his parents were not looking. His brothers and sisters tattled on him. "Momma and Daddy, he's got his school clothes on, he's plannin' to go to school," they would say.[5] His parents seldom stopped him, though. Willie Mae Lewis saw from an early age that John was different. She believed that her son had been touched by the Lord.[6]

In 1954, when John was fourteen, the U.S. Supreme Court, in its decision in *Brown* v. *Board of Education of Topeka, Kansas*, ruled that segregated ("separate but equal") schools were unconstitutional. "We rejoiced. It was like a day of jubilee," Lewis remembered.[7] He thought that his years of shabby schools and second-hand books were over. Now he could get a real high school education. It did not happen. In many states, including Alabama, local authorities defied the law of the land and kept their segregated and unequal schools. John was bitterly disappointed.

The year after the *Brown* decision, John was electrified by the news of the bus boycott in Montgomery, a city only fifty miles away. "I read *everything* about what was happening there, and it was really one of the most exciting . . . things to me to see just a few miles away the black folks of Montgomery sticking together, refusing to ride the segregated buses," he said.[8]

The boycott began when Rosa Parks, a seamstress and civil rights activist, refused to give up her seat in the first row of the "colored" section of a city bus. A white man was standing, so Parks, who was black, was expected to move. After she was arrested, the African-American community united in protest. They decided to walk and carpool rather than continue to sit in the back of the bus. Eventually, the bus company was forced by the courts to end racial segregation.

The boycott was led by the Montgomery Improvement Association (MIA), whose president was the young pastor of an African-American church, the Reverend Martin Luther King, Jr. Dr. King was already John's idol. Since receiving his first Bible at age five, John had known he wanted to become a preacher. His devout Baptist parents encouraged him. One day, John was listening to a local radio station when a new preacher was featured. It was Dr. King. He delivered a sermon that related the apostle Paul's writings to the American racial situation. "His message [made] religion something real," Lewis recalled.[9] King's leadership of the boycott "took the words that I'd heard him preach over the radio and put them into action in a way that set the course of my life from that point on," Lewis said. The Montgomery Bus Boycott "changed my life."[10]

Not long afterward, riots broke out at the University of Alabama. An African-American student, Autherine Lucy, attempted to enroll in classes there.

She won a court order forcing the school to admit her. The university's president then expelled her, claiming it was for her own safety. "Thinking about [her] courage," said Lewis, "I became even more convinced that I had to make myself part of all this."[11]

Twelve days later, John Lewis preached his first sermon in his local church. His picture soon appeared in the "Negro section" of the *Montgomery Advertiser*. He was called the "boy preacher from Pike County."[12] John was only sixteen. Though he was ordained as a minister shortly afterward, John longed to study theology in college. His dream was to attend Morehouse College in Atlanta, Georgia, where Dr. King had gone. When he sent for a college catalog, however, he saw that it was far too expensive for him.

One day, John's mother brought home a Baptist magazine from the orphanage where she sometimes did cleaning. It contained an advertisement for a college called the American Baptist Theological Seminary, in Nashville, Tennessee. The school charged no tuition; all students worked their way through the school. John applied and was accepted.

In 1957, John Lewis became the first member of his household to graduate from secondary school. That fall, at age seventeen, he left home for college, traveling alone by bus. Everything he owned, his clothing and a Bible, was packed in a footlocker. His uncle Otis surprised him with the gift of a hundred dollar bill. It was more money than John had ever held in his hand before.

At college "[I] got a job working in the kitchen, washing pots and pans," he said. "[They were] huge pots, dirty pots . . . the biggest pots and pans I had ever seen in my life."[13] During his freshman year, he made friends, studied, and read everything he could on the growing civil rights movement. He tried to organize a student chapter of the National Association for the Advancement of Colored People (NAACP), the group that had fought and won the *Brown* case. The college president forbade it, fearing that it would anger whites and the school would lose white financial support as a result.

Lewis then got the idea of succeeding where Autherine Lucy had failed. He would become the first black student to attend a white Alabama college. He applied to Troy State College, near his home, as a transfer student. But his application was ignored. Lewis began to write and call the Montgomery Improvement Association, asking the group to support him in bringing a lawsuit to force integration, as Autherine Lucy had. The Reverend Ralph Abernathy, Dr. King's right-hand man, was impressed. He paid Lewis's bus fare to Montgomery so that he could meet Dr. King and speak to him personally.

Civil rights organizations chose well-educated, well-spoken students for their test cases. That did not describe John Lewis. The inadequacy of his secondary school had made it necessary for him to take extra math and English courses to prepare for college-level work. His manners and speech were very unpolished. Worst of all, he spoke with a stammer.

"I was petrified," Lewis remembered of his first meeting with Dr. King. He could hardly speak, but it did not matter because King and Abernathy did all the talking. They warned him of the danger he would face, not just for himself but for his family. They could face harassment, loss of jobs, even physical danger. Lewis managed to nod to show he was still determined. The Montgomery Improvement Association agreed to press the case if Lewis's parents would consent; he was still a minor. Lewis left the meeting starstruck. "I could have floated back [home]," he remembered.[14] Unfortunately, his parents were too afraid to agree. Disappointed but understanding their position, Lewis returned to the seminary for his sophomore year.

3

THE SIT-INS

In the fall of 1958, John Lewis began to attend a series of church workshops on nonviolent protest and resistance. The teacher was a young African-American minister named James Lawson, who had studied nonviolence when he was a missionary in India. There, Mohandas Gandhi, an attorney who led hundreds of thousands of Indians in nonviolent protest, had forced the British Empire to grant India its independence. Back in the United States, Lawson led discussions of the history of civil disobedience as a way of causing social change. He talked about the Montgomery bus boycott and the emerging civil rights movement. Its leader, the Reverend Martin Luther King, Jr., was another admirer of Gandhi.

Most of those attending the workshops were college students. "The workshops became almost like [another college course] to students like me," Lewis said. "It was the most important thing we were doing."[1] As he had during the bus boycott, Lewis found himself at a turning point in his life. "I'd finally found the setting and the subject that spoke to everything that had been stirring in my soul for so long."[2]

Lawson arranged for some of his students, including Lewis, to attend a weekend meeting at the Highlander Folk School. Both blacks and whites gathered at this unique, integrated workshop in the Tennessee mountains. One staff member gave the opinion that Lewis did not speak well enough to lead others. Another staff member, the legendary voting rights activist Septima Clark, disagreed. "What difference [does] it make?" she asked. The people he needed to lead already understood him, she believed, because he was one of them.[3] He spoke the way they did.

Finally, the time came for theory to become practice. Workshop members began to plan nonviolent actions to challenge segregation. African-American shoppers had long resented being refused service at store lunch counters. Only a few feet away were cash registers where their money was gladly accepted, regardless of their race. So the Nashville Christian Leadership Council, a group of ministers and church members pushing for civil rights, requested in 1959 that restaurants and lunch counters serve everyone. The store owners refused.

The students in Lawson's workshop swung into action. They began practicing for nonviolent protests they called "sit-ins." They hoped the protests would force lunch counters to integrate. Some students would act the roles of customers, asking for service at segregated lunch counters. Others would pretend to be against integration, jeering, poking, and spitting on them. So committed did the workshop members become that, led by Lewis and his friend Diane Nash, they formed an organization called the Nashville Student Movement, to support the local civil rights plan.

Finally, the students were ready to try a test sit-in at a real lunch counter. When they were refused service, the students simply got up and left. Modest as it was, this defiance thrilled Lewis. The college semester was about to end. After Christmas vacation, he and his friends would take the next step. They would sit down and stay there.[4]

But before Lewis could act, national headlines broke the news that on February 1, 1960, four black

Many restaurants closed down rather than serve African Americans. A restaurant owner in Albany, Georgia, posted this defiant sign in his window.

college freshmen had staged their own sit-in at a Greensboro, North Carolina, five-and-dime store. The four were not connected to the Nashville activists. Lewis and Nash were not resentful that they would not be the first. "It was something out there tracking people down," Lewis said. "It was hate and history coming together. The spirit of history just tracked us down and used us."[5] Lewis and his friends believed that the time was right for things to change. They believed that helping to cause that change was their destiny.

The sit-in movement quickly spread to other southern cities and towns. The Nashville students speeded up their timetable. Lawson gave crash courses in nonviolence to the hundreds of students who were eager to join the original group. On the eve of their first sit-in, planned for February 13, 1960, Lewis was unable to sleep. "There's a stirring inside . . . the sense of a power beyond you, of a calling, a mission. That's a strong feeling," he remembered.[6]

They awoke that Saturday morning to a snowfall, unusual for Nashville. As Lewis described it: "The students were dressed like they were on their way to church."[7] Two by two, 124 of them walked downtown. They spread themselves out in groups of twenty-five among the major five-and-dime stores along Nashville's main street. The members of Lewis's group quietly seated themselves at Woolworth's second-floor lunch counter. A waitress who saw them stopped and stared.[8] She was soon followed by another store employee, who propped a hand-lettered sign in front of them. "COUNTER CLOSED," it read. Then the lights went out. The students read and did homework by light from the store's windows until six o'clock in the evening, when the demonstration was scheduled to end.

Five days later, hundreds of students sat-in as more

stores were targeted. Many of the newcomers had received little or no training in nonviolence. They did not understand the discipline the original demonstrators observed. They expected to be able to smoke and chat at the lunch counters. Lewis drew up a list of guidelines for them. This became known as the Nashville Student Code, and it served as a model for the movement:

1. Don't strike back or curse if abused.
2. Don't laugh out.
3. Don't hold conversations with floor workers.
4. Don't block entrances to the store and aisles.
5. Show yourself courteous and friendly at all times.
6. Sit straight and always face the counter.
7. Remember love and nonviolence.
8. May God bless each of you.[9]

A sympathetic white minister had heard a rumor that white hoodlums planned to attack the demonstrators on February 27. He heard that the police would arrest the demonstrators, not the attackers. The minister warned the students.

The rumor the minister had heard was right. A group of young white men attacked and beat the sit-in participants, particularly the women. They even put lighted cigarettes down their backs and in their hair. In another store, students were squirted with ketchup and mustard, then pulled off their stools and kicked until they were bloody. A national television camera crew

At this lunch-counter sit-in, angry whites poured sugar, ketchup, and mustard over the heads of the protesters.

captured this scene on film for the nightly news. As predicted, the students, not their attackers, were arrested. As Lewis and the others were led out by the police, they sang "We Shall Overcome." "It was really happening," Lewis remembered. "What I'd imagined for so long, the drama of good and evil playing itself out."[10]

African Americans in Nashville united in the students' defense and raised $50,000 in one day as bail money. African-American attorney Z. Alexander Looby argued at their trial that the students were victims of assault, not criminals. As the attorney made his case, the judge turned his back and stared at the wall, then quickly found the students guilty. Most of them, including Lewis, decided to serve their sentences as a moral protest rather than pay the fines the judge imposed.

"Growing up in the rural South, it was not the thing to do . . . to go to jail," Lewis remembered. "It would bring shame and disgrace on the family. Me, I'll tell you, it was like being involved in a holy crusade. It became a badge of honor."[11] Lewis's family reacted with horror. "My mother wrote me a letter and said, 'Get out of the movement,'" he recalled, "but I couldn't."[12]

African-American residents started a boycott of downtown businesses, refusing to shop at stores that discriminated. "No fashions for Easter" was their slogan. They marched in front of stores, urging shoppers not to go in. As the holiday approached, instead of being filled with shoppers buying new clothes, the stores remained empty. Panicky merchants began to press for a settlement. The white hoodlums struck back, attacking boycotters outside the stores.

Then, on April 19, 1960, at 5:30 A.M., attorney Looby's home was firebombed and destroyed. A block away, the blast blew 147 windows out of Nashville's main black hospital. The whole city, black and white, was shocked and angry. Even the mayor denounced the violence. That same morning, three thousand adults and young people staged a silent protest march on City Hall. "I had never seen anything like [it]," Lewis remembered. "This was the first such mass [civil rights] march in the history of America. . . . The only sound was the sound of our footsteps, all those feet."[13]

On the steps of City Hall, Mayor Ben West met the protesters. Diane Nash, who led the march, confronted him with a list of questions. A few rows back, John Lewis listened. "Mayor West," Nash asked, "do you feel it is wrong to discriminate against a person solely on the basis of their race or color?" The mayor bravely responded that, speaking as a man, not a politician, he did not think it morally right.[14]

Nash persisted. "Then, Mayor, do you recommend that the lunch counters be desegregated?"

"Yes," said West.[15]

The next day, Nashville's newspaper headlines read, "Mayor Says to Integrate Counters." That was all the merchants needed; they gave in. On May 10, 1960, African Americans sat down to be served at lunch counters for the first time in the city's history.

That spring, sit-ins at Nashville lunch counters were stopped to allow integration to take place. Lewis and other students devoted much of their time to traveling to colleges and speaking to campus groups about their nonviolent resistance to segregation. By

Lewis helped teach other students the rules of nonviolent protests.

the fall of 1960, though, the students were ready to take aim at some of the other Nashville establishments that were still racially divided. They targeted fast-food restaurants and cafeterias in Nashville for more sit-ins.

Next the students turned their attention to movie theaters. Some of the theaters refused to admit blacks. Others seated black patrons apart from whites. In February 1961, the students began picketing one Nashville theater after another, pressuring them to integrate. Again, menacing white hoodlums threatened the pickets and rioting was feared.

One day, Lewis and some other students met to plan their picketing strategy. The group's adult advisers pushed them to negotiate rather than provoke violence. As the debate raged, Lewis was repeatedly asked his opinion. Every time, he would respond simply, "We're gonna march tonight." One of the adults accused Lewis of risking the lives of demonstrators out of pride, bullheadedness, and his own sin. In the silence that followed, Lewis sat smiling. Finally he answered, "Okay, I'm a sinner. We're gonna march."[16]

Victory was won in March, when the movie theaters gave in to the pressure to integrate their seating. Not long afterward, Lewis heard about a plan to integrate interstate buses. He knew immediately that he was destined to be a part of the Freedom Ride. "Somehow, the Spirit of History was putting its hands on my life again," he said.[17] Lewis, who had already faced verbal and physical abuse in his fight for integration, would encounter even greater dangers in the months to come.

Lewis and his fellow Freedom Riders traveled without trouble through towns in Virginia and North Carolina. But on May 9, Lewis met violence in Rock Hill, South Carolina.

4

SNCC

fter being beaten up in Rock Hill, South Carolina, John Lewis left the Freedom Ride for a few days. He flew to Philadelphia, Pennsylvania, where the American Friends Service Committee was considering his application for foreign service. The Friends interviewed him and awarded him a post in India to begin later that summer. Lewis then flew to Nashville. From there, he intended to travel by car to rejoin the Freedom Ride in Birmingham, Alabama.

Lewis landed in Nashville on Saturday, May 13. Meanwhile, his fellow Freedom Riders had continued without him from South Carolina to Atlanta, Georgia.

They dined there with the Reverend Martin Luther King, Jr., and other civil rights leaders. No further incidents had marred the rest of their journey through South Carolina and Georgia. Toasts were proposed in celebration of the Freedom Ride's successful first seven hundred miles. Nevertheless, Dr. King feared that violence lay ahead. He pulled aside a reporter who was accompanying the group. "You will never make it through Alabama," he whispered.[1]

Lewis learned how right Dr. King was the next day. Before leaving Nashville by car to rejoin the Freedom Ride, Lewis heard by radio that a bus carrying Freedom Riders was burning in Anniston, Alabama. If not for his interview in Philadelphia, Lewis would have been on that bus. A racist gang had surrounded the bus, slashing its tires, breaking its windows, and hurling a firebomb inside. Luckily, the passengers had escaped before the gas tank blew up.

And there was more. The Freedom Riders had split up, with half taking another bus. Thugs on board this bus beat them during the ride to Anniston. Still, they continued to Birmingham, not knowing what had become of their comrades in the other bus. At the Birmingham bus terminal, a huge mob met them. For fifteen minutes, the Freedom Riders were beaten bloody. No police appeared. Police chief Eugene "Bull" Connor later explained that it was Mother's Day, and all his officers wanted to be with their mothers.

Sheriff "Bull" Connor used Mother's Day as an excuse for not protecting the Freedom Riders from mob violence in Birmingham, Alabama.

The violence shattered CORE's plan. Most of the Freedom Riders were hospitalized. CORE decided to abandon the ride as too dangerous. The remaining participants would fly to New Orleans, which had been their last planned stop.

Lewis realized that if peaceful protest could be stopped by violence, equal rights could never be achieved in states that used brute force. The students of Nashville, staring danger in the face, vowed to continue the Freedom Ride. The Student Nonviolent Coordinating Committee (SNCC) chose ten volunteers. John Lewis, one of the chosen, would become the only person to both begin and end the Freedom Ride. All the new Freedom Riders said tearful good-byes to their friends and relatives. Some of them had written their wills.

Lewis's fellow activist Diane Nash stayed in Nashville to coordinate the plan. She telephoned civil rights workers in Birmingham. They feared their phones might be tapped and spoke in code. A shipment of ten "chickens," Nash said, would arrive the next day.[2]

Lewis was deep in thought as he rode the bus from Nashville back to his home state of Alabama. He remembered a childhood trip with his uncle Otis to Buffalo, New York. His mother had cooked and packed all the food they would need. They would not be allowed to eat in restaurants along the way till they reached the North. But worst was being turned away from rest rooms. He hated the sight of adults forced to relieve themselves by the side of the road. He was now taking part in the Freedom Ride for his family, as well as for justice.[3]

On Wednesday, May 17, 1961, the bus carrying ten "chickens" was stopped by Birmingham city police. An officer inspected the passengers' tickets. He laughed. "Y'all are Freedom Riders," he said.[4] As the bus pulled into the terminal, Lewis noticed more reporters than he had ever seen before. Now the whole country was watching. Police detained the Freedom Riders all day; first in the bus, its windows darkened from the outside, then in an empty terminal.

Police chief "Bull" Connor announced that the Freedom Riders were being arrested for their own protection. He held them in jail for two days. Then, after midnight, he loaded them into cars, drove them to the Alabama/Tennessee border, and stopped. "This is where you'll be gettin' out," he told them. It was the middle of the night. The students feared they had been set up for lynching by the Ku Klux Klan, the white supremacist hate group.[5]

The students picked up their bags and tramped out into the country by moonlight. They would have the best chance of finding a friendly African-American family farther from town. At last they came to a small house. It was nearly dawn. An elderly African-American man answered their knock. Lewis told him they were Freedom Riders and needed help. The frightened man tried to close the door, but his wife stopped him. "Honey," she said. "Let them in."[6] Miraculously, these poor people had a telephone. Lewis called Diane Nash and asked for a car to pick them up. There was no question that they would return to Birmingham to continue the ride.

Nash was pleased. She told them "eleven other 'packages' had already been 'shipped.'"[7] Now there were twenty-one Freedom Riders. They reunited in Birmingham and planned to ride the three o'clock bus to Montgomery, Alabama.

By now, the Freedom Ride had captured the nation's attention. An angry U.S. Attorney General Robert Kennedy, brother of President John F.

Kennedy, tried to force the governor of Alabama to guarantee safe passage for the bus to Montgomery. But the governor also went to court to get an order, or injunction, declaring the Freedom Ride illegal as a disturbance of the peace.

At 8:30 A.M. on Saturday, May 20, a Greyhound bus pulled out of the Birmingham terminal, headed for Montgomery. The Freedom Riders rode alone on it. Police cars, with flashing lights and screaming sirens, surrounded the bus. At the city limits, the Alabama highway patrol took over. Every fifteen miles a different patrol car took over. A state police airplane flew overhead. Then, shortly before Montgomery, "all signs of protection disappeared," Lewis said. "There was no plane, no patrol cars. And when we arrived at the bus station, it was just an eerie, just a strange feeling. It was so quiet."[8]

The Freedom Ride was now major news. A group of reporters waited on the platform in Montgomery. They moved forward with their cameras and microphones as the bus doors opened. The Freedom Riders had chosen Lewis as their spokesman. He exited the bus first. A reporter from *Life* magazine began a question, then stopped. He followed Lewis's stare. Hundreds of white men, women, and children swarmed onto the platform. They swung baseball bats, chains, and tire irons, their faces contorted with rage. "*Git them . . . GIT them,*" they chanted.[9] The white mob

This Freedom Ride bus was attacked and firebombed by a racist mob near Anniston, Alabama. But no amount of violence could stop the Freedom Riders.

snatched cameras from the press and used them as weapons. Lewis tried to get his fellow Freedom Riders to stand together. He shouted directions to a nearby church, where they could take sanctuary. The attackers' screams drowned him out. One by one, the rioters picked off members of the group and dragged them away. Lewis could see their legs disappear into the mob. This "was all happening at once," he remembered, "within seconds."[10]

Then the crowd turned on Lewis. He felt his suitcase wrenched from his hand. Attackers surrounded him. Someone used the suitcase to pound him. Then a tremendous blow landed on his head. His knees buckled. Everything went black. "We saw John Lewis lying on the ground, blood streaming from his head," another student remembered.[11]

A few Freedom Riders escaped into the basement of the building next door. Others, mostly women, made it to a row of cabs and sped away. The mob continued to kick and pound the injured. Lewis felt consciousness returning. Was he going to die? he wondered. "At least I was true to myself," he thought. Then he heard a voice say, "There'll be no killing here today." Two shots rang out. Floyd Mann, the Alabama public safety director, fired his pistol into the air to disperse the attackers. He pulled men off the fallen Freedom Riders.[12]

Nearby, a man stood over Lewis, who still lay on the

ground. This man had not come to help the Freedom Riders. He read out loud from a document in his hands. It was the Alabama attorney general, reading the court injunction that had been granted to stop the Freedom Ride. Lewis dragged himself, bleeding, to a taxi stand. The cabbie drove him to a local African-American doctor, who bandaged his head.

The injunction lasted only four days. The Freedom Riders went to court and succeeded in getting it lifted on May 22, 1961. John Lewis and other civil rights leaders met with reporters. Lewis still wore a large, cross-shaped bandage on the back of his head, from having his skull cracked in the Montgomery bus station. They announced that the Freedom Ride would continue. Their next stop would be in Mississippi.

At the Jackson, Mississippi, bus terminal, Lewis and his comrades used the white rest rooms and lunch counters. Police swarmed in, accusing them of "trespassing." Arrested by a police officer while using a urinal in the white rest room, Lewis barely had time to zip up.

The Freedom Riders were tried, and each was sentenced to six weeks in prison. For two weeks they were held at county jails. Then, in the dead of night, guards rousted them from their cots and herded them into windowless truck trailers. "The guards kept their guns drawn all the time and they taunted us, told us we'd be killed," Lewis remembered.[13] After a two-hour drive, the trucks stopped deep in the countryside. Lewis saw miles of barbed wire fences. He realized he was about to become a prisoner at the notorious Parchman State Penitentiary.

"We were forced to strip naked and wait for an hour and a half, without knowing what was going to happen to us," Lewis said. "For the first time in my life, I was literally . . . terrified."[14] Guards placed them two to a cell. They received their clothing rations: an undershirt and shorts. They saw no one but their cellmates, except when showering twice a week.

Still, the guards never touched them. Though the Freedom Riders did not know it, the governor of Mississippi had ordered a hands-off policy to avoid bad publicity. This caused the guards great frustration. Lewis heard that they complained they had no way to stop the Freedom Riders from singing if they could not "go upside their heads."[15] As always, the students sang freedom songs to keep up their spirits. "We used to rock the jails [at Parchman]," Lewis said. "The [criminal] prisoners downstairs used to sing with us."[16]

While in jail, Lewis wrote to officials at American Baptist Theological Seminary explaining that he would miss his college graduation in June. He also wrote to the American Friends Service Committee to cancel his assignment in India. He realized that his calling would be in his own country. Finally, Lewis and his fellow Freedom Riders were released from prison on July 7, 1961.

After the Freedom Ride, Lewis became alienated from his family. "[They] never understood why I had become involved," he remembered. "They thought I was just going bad. . . . I did go back to Alabama to see my folks for a few days later that summer, but I needed contact with people who understood and supported me. . . . The movement . . . became my family."[17]

Lewis also realized that he no longer wished to become a minister, another disappointment to his parents. Fortunately, he and other Freedom Riders were awarded college scholarships by Dr. King's new organization, the Southern Christian Leadership Conference. Lewis chose to attend Fisk University in Nashville to study for a second college degree, this time in philosophy. He took a light course load so he could devote most of his time to the civil rights movement.

The sit-ins continued in Nashville. Though integration of lunch counters and theaters had been a great victory, many other public places remained segregated. Lewis and a new group of activists spent 1961 "marching through the Yellow Pages," said Lewis.[18] They targeted stores, restaurants, bowling alleys, skating rinks—businesses of all kinds. Many of his friends, including Diane Nash, had either graduated or gone to work full-time for civil rights organizations. The Nashville Student Movement had by now become a

By his early twenties, Lewis had transformed from a stammering teenager into a well-spoken young man with an unshakable commitment to civil rights.

branch of the Student Nonviolent Coordinating Committee. SNCC (pronounced "snick") had been formed to link student protest movements all over the country.

By the spring of 1962, twenty-two-year-old John Lewis was a far different person from the teenager who had joined the civil rights movement. Gone was the stammering, unpolished country boy. Mary King, a white SNCC member, described him as "poised, modest, self-confident and clear-minded" though "a little shy."[19] Lewis was elected to SNCC's Executive Committee in 1962. The Reverend Martin Luther King, Jr., nominated him for the SCLC board the same year, saying that Lewis "was transforming the face of Nashville."[20]

Lewis's SNCC colleagues showed that they held him in high esteem when they elected him the group's chairman in June 1963. The chairman's main job would be fund-raising, which required much traveling and public speaking. Yet the group needed a chairman who was an activist as well. The group thought John Lewis combined both qualities. "I don't think it was possible to frighten John, so intense was his commitment," wrote Mary King. "The ardor of his example made him acceptable to everyone to chair SNCC, including those who were more impatient."[21] Lewis himself simply felt that the spirit of history was using him again. "I sensed a power at work that was much larger than any of us," he said.[22] Just a few credits short of his degree at Fisk, Lewis dropped out and moved to Atlanta, home of SNCC's headquarters.

Almost immediately, Lewis was thrust onto the national stage when Dr. King announced plans for a mass march on Washington in 1963. Lewis would represent SNCC in planning the event and would give one of the major speeches there. A. Philip Randolph, one of the march's organizers, was the head of the railroad porters' union and the grand old man of the civil rights movement. Randolph had dreamed of a mass march for racial justice since the 1940s. Now his dream was about to come true. He and the other major civil rights leaders, including Lewis, set a date: August 28.

President Kennedy sent for the "big six"—King, Randolph, Lewis, and the heads of the NAACP, CORE, and the Urban League. As usual, the twenty-three-year-old Lewis was the youngest person present. "It was mind-blowing for me to be there," he said. "Exactly one week after being elected chairman of SNCC, here I was at the White House."[23] Kennedy had hoped to talk the leaders out of marching but quickly saw that that was futile. So he spent the meeting urging them to back the new civil rights bill that he had just proposed to Congress. Lewis listened quietly, absorbing everything about the amazing scene.

"That summer was a whirlwind for me," he

remembered.[24] As SNCC chairman, he crisscrossed the South, visiting SNCC projects, making speeches, taking part in demonstrations, giving interviews, making plans. He visited Greenwood, Mississippi; Pine Bluff, Arkansas; Somerville, Tennessee; Danville, Virginia; Cambridge, Maryland; and a dozen other cities and towns.

For the March on Washington, Lewis prepared a speech that challenged the federal government to use its full power to assure equal rights. Until then, the Kennedy administration had been compromising with southern states instead of standing firm on equal rights. For example, Kennedy's bill would allow southern states to continue requiring tests for literacy and knowledge of civics before allowing voters to register. SNCC opposed any literacy requirement. "[We] took the position that the only qualification for being able to register to vote should be that of age and residence," Lewis argued. "It was never [our] design to come to Washington to support [Kennedy's bill]."[25]

Lewis consulted other SNCC staffers, who advised him on what to include and strengthen in his speech. When finished writing it, he was satisfied that it was good and strong. Then, the night before the march, he was asked to make some changes. Lewis was shocked. A SNCC staffer had distributed copies of the final draft to the press. When several other march speakers read it, they felt it was too militant. They threatened to leave the march if Lewis did not change his speech. Lewis compromised on several points and believed the matter was settled.

The next morning, the leaders of the march met with some senators and congressmen who supported their cause. While they were still meeting at the Capitol, however, impatient crowds of marchers were surging forward without them. As the leaders rushed to join them, their cars were blocked by the mass of thousands of marchers. The leaders jumped from their

President John F. Kennedy, fourth from right, invited civil rights leaders to the White House after the March on Washington in 1963. John Lewis is third from left, next to the Reverend Martin Luther King, Jr. A. Philip Randolph is in the center.

cars and squeezed into the line. "It was truly awesome, the most incredible thing I'd ever seen in my life," Lewis remembered.[26] The crush of people propelled the leaders to the Mall, the site of the main rally and speeches.

As the speakers gathered inside the Lincoln Memorial at the end of the Mall, the controversy over Lewis's speech began again. He did not want to make any more changes, but Dr. King and Randolph asked him personally to tone down his language for the sake of unity. Out of respect for their leadership and service to the movement, he relented.

Randolph introduced him. "Brother Lewis," he said, stepping aside to let the younger man take the podium. As Lewis looked out at the hundreds of thousands of people filling the Mall, he felt "great humility and incredible fear." At first, his voice almost failed him. But then, "I quickly caught the feeling," he remembered. "The call and response, just like in church. The crowd was with me."[27]

Even his toned-down speech was considered by many to be the most hard-hitting of the day. "By the force of our demands," Lewis said, "our determination and our numbers, we shall splinter the desegregated South into a thousand pieces and put them back together in the image of God and democracy. We must say 'Wake up, America. *Wake up!!!* For we cannot stop and we *will* not be patient.'"[28]

The March on Washington for Jobs and Freedom has come down in history as one of the defining events of the civil rights movement. Virtually everyone has heard and been stirred by Dr. King's "I Have a Dream" speech. For Lewis and others in SNCC, however, the march was most memorable for the sight of 250,000 people of all colors united to call for racial justice. For the first time, one SNCC member said, the ordinary African Americans SNCC was struggling to organize in the South realized "they were not alone, that there really were people in the nation who cared what happened to them."[29]

5

THE STRUGGLE FOR THE VOTE

t is hard to believe that in the 1960s, Americans died for the right to vote. But it is true. Mary King, in SNCC's communications office, documented hundreds of beatings, bombings, arsons, evictions, job losses, and even murders of blacks by whites. Why did this violence happen? Simply because these courageous men and women tried to register to vote. Despite the Fifteenth Amendment to the U.S. Constitution in 1870, which stated that voting rights could not be denied by race, few blacks in the Deep South had been allowed to vote.

The whites in power used several methods to keep

blacks from voting. Seven southern states added "grandfather clauses" to their constitutions. These specified that only people whose grandfathers had voted before the Civil War would be allowed to vote. The grandfather clause had been declared unconstitutional in 1915 but was still invoked in some places. Another was the poll tax, essentially a fee paid to vote. Although the Twenty-fourth Amendment to the Constitution stated that poll taxes could not be imposed in federal elections, most southern states still required them in state and local elections. Some southern states also made voters register twice, once for federal elections and once for state and local elections.

A third way to limit voting in the South at that time was the literacy test. This required a certain level of education to vote or the passing of a written test. (State poll taxes and literacy tests were eventually declared unconstitutional.) A fourth method was limiting the places, days, and hours for voter registration. Voters could not register by mail. They had to apply in person at the county courthouse, and the office was open only a few hours a month. Poor blacks often had no transportation to a distant county courthouse or could not take time off from work. In addition, many counties published the names of voter registrants in the newspaper. This created more problems for black voters. White employers and landlords could then fire or evict those who registered.

Finally, sheer terror tactics were used to deter voters. In 1961, a Mississippi farmer named Herbert Lee was shot dead by a white state legislator for urging blacks to register to vote. He would not be the last to die. White racists were most vicious in the many southern counties where blacks outnumbered whites. Clearly, if blacks were allowed to vote there, white racist politicians would lose their offices and their power.

By late 1963, SNCC had focused most of its energy on voter registration. When Lewis used the slogan "one man, one vote" in his March on Washington speech, it became the rallying cry of the voter registration movement.

One of the flashpoints of this movement was Selma, Alabama, where barely 1 percent of the African-American population had been allowed to register. Selma's Dallas County Courthouse was open for voter registration only two days per month. SNCC dubbed these "Freedom Mondays." Hundreds of African Americans lined up to register on these days. Their single-file line stretched around the block, surrounded by state troopers, sheriff's deputies, and "citizens' posses" consisting of any white man with a gun who wished to join. These men harassed and sometimes beat those waiting to register.

Beginning in 1963, Lewis made regular trips to Selma to lend his support. One day, carrying a sign reading "One Man, One Vote," Lewis led a demonstration to the courthouse. Troopers arrested him and his fellow demonstrators for "unlawful assembly." They used electric cattle prods to herd the demonstrators into buses, then confined them in filthy converted chicken coops.

Two weeks later, on Freedom Monday, Lewis returned. Three hundred African Americans lined up outside the courthouse, planning to apply to register to vote. They stood all day in the hot summer sun, not allowed to leave the line to eat, drink, or go to the bathroom. SNCC workers were arrested for trying to supply them with food and water. "At the end of the day only about five people had made it in to take the so-called literacy tests," Lewis remembered. "I can never forget that day."[1] Across the street at the federal building, U.S. Justice Department employees and FBI agents simply watched.

In nearby Mississippi, civil rights workers tried another tactic. They planned a "Freedom Vote" to coincide with the national Election Day in November 1963. Only 5 percent of Mississippi's African Americans had been permitted to register to vote. These people could cast real ballots. But civil rights activists planned a mock election to be held alongside the real one. Activists "ran" for statewide office and invited unregistered blacks to cast their votes. The mock election would allow black Mississippians to see what it would be like to express their will through the ballot box. It would also discredit white Mississippians who claimed that local blacks did not really wish to vote, that they were only being spurred on by "outside agitators." Ballot boxes were placed in barbershops, beauty parlors, stores, and churches. Ninety thousand black Mississippians cast ballots in the Freedom Vote. "The campaign was an incredible success," Lewis remembered.[2]

Even this mock vote aroused brutal opposition. Civil rights workers documented more than one hundred incidents of police interference with the Freedom Vote. Lewis was organizing the mock vote in Roseland, Mississippi, on Election Day. Local police there seized him and escorted him out of town. But this was only the beginning of an intense effort to win voting rights for Mississippi African Americans.

Shortly after the election, on November 22, President John F. Kennedy was assassinated. Lewis said he was "devastated."[3] Lewis believed that Kennedy had come to feel that inequality of the races was a "defining moral issue" and would have supported civil rights activists in the future.[4] The new president, Lyndon B. Johnson, was a southerner, a Texan. President Johnson appeared before Congress urging it to pass the Civil Rights Act as a memorial to the murdered president. Lewis said he found this "encouraging," but otherwise took a wait-and-see attitude.[5]

Lewis joined a sit-in campaign in Atlanta, his new

hometown, in December 1963 and January 1964. The Georgia capital considered itself a model of good race relations, but it lagged behind Nashville in integration of public places. In a novel tactic, Lewis and other SNCC members bought stock in a segregated restaurant chain, then staged a sit-in at one of its restaurants. When they were arrested, the company looked ridiculous. It had denied service to its part-owners.

A national human rights group, which planned to come to Atlanta to study race relations, asked SNCC to suspend demonstrations during its visit to avoid embarrassing the nation. Lewis refused. African Americans, he retorted, had "been embarrassed a long time" by segregation.[6]

But most of SNCC's energies in 1964 were concentrated upon preparations for its most ambitious project yet: "Freedom Summer." This would be an all-out campaign to register African Americans in Mississippi to vote. For the first time, SNCC planned to recruit hundreds of white college students to help. Some would go door-to-door, talking to prospective voters. Some would drive local citizens to county courthouses to register. Others would teach in "Freedom Schools," preparing adults for literacy tests and giving educational enrichment to children. Lewis crisscrossed the country. He spoke on dozens of campuses, including the nation's most elite universities, seeking volunteers. SNCC, though always open to both blacks and whites, had been 70 percent African-American until then. "Bringing these white kids in would be like bringing in a spotlight," Lewis admitted.[7]

White Mississippi prepared, too. Governor Paul Johnson announced that the state highway patrol force would be doubled that summer. Police departments stockpiled weapons. The city of Jackson even bought a tank. The Ku Klux Klan burned crosses in sixty-four of the state's eighty-two counties in one night.

Lewis believed that a project as big as Freedom Summer would force the federal government's hand. SNCC hoped that Washington would take control of voter registration in Mississippi when it saw that whites were fighting against it. "Before the Negro people get the right to vote, there will have to be a massive confrontation," said Lewis. He was hopeful, saying that "1964 could really be the year for Mississippi."[8] Still, he did not fool himself that there would be no violence. "Out of this conflict, this division and chaos, will come something positive," he said.[9] He was right, but the price would be high.

A member of the Jackson, Mississippi, police force demonstrates how he will be able to fire a weapon from inside the tank his department bought to prepare for "Freedom Summer."

6

FREEDOM
SUMMER

hat was a long summer, that summer of '64,"
Lewis remembered. "Intense. Confusing.
Painful. So hopeful in the beginning, and so
heartbreaking in the end."[1]

Half the Freedom Summer volunteers arrived in
Oxford, Ohio, on June 13, 1964, for training. Lewis and
other SNCC staffers explained Mississippi's history of
racism and repression. Through role-playing exercises,
the volunteers prepared for the hostility and name-
calling they would face. Trainers drilled them on
safety precautions and stressed the possibility of
violence. "I may be killed," James Forman, SNCC

executive secretary, said bluntly. "You may be killed."[2]

Following their training, the first group left for Mississippi. When the second group arrived in Ohio the next week, they heard shocking news. A member of the first group, after just one day in Mississippi, was already missing and feared dead, as were the two other volunteers who had been with him. "Not already," thought an anguished Lewis when he heard the news.[3]

Andrew Goodman, a white New York college student, had disappeared along with two other civil rights workers: Mickey Schwerner, also a white New Yorker, and James Chaney, a black Mississippian. The three had gone to inspect the fire-gutted ruins of a church that was being used as a Freedom School. A local lawman, Deputy Sheriff Cecil Price, reported that he had arrested the three men for speeding in Philadelphia, Mississippi. Price claimed that he had released them late that night after they paid a $20 fine. But the men had never telephoned SNCC headquarters upon their release, as they were strictly required to do.

Three days after the disappearance, Lewis arrived in Philadelphia, Mississippi, with a caravan of thirty-five prominent civil rights activists. At the city limits, Sheriff Lawrence Rainey, Price's boss, stopped their cars and escorted them directly to the courthouse. Lewis and three others met with county officials. They demanded to visit the church ruins and the site where the victims' car had just been found, empty and burned. The sheriff forbade this, saying that both sites were private property. Lewis countered that he thought they were both on public land. "Your thoughts are nonsense," barked the sheriff.

The head of the Congress of Racial Equality then asked to see the car, which was owned by his organization. The county attorney denied this request, too, claiming their inspection of the car might destroy evidence useful in solving the crime. "If there has been a crime," he quickly added. Lewis and the others left, feeling angry but helpless.[4] Lewis and some friends returned secretly that evening and searched the area where the car had been found. Nothing turned up, but at least they felt they had done something.

White Mississippians denounced the disappearance as a hoax or publicity stunt designed to draw attention to Freedom Summer and embarrass the state. President Johnson ordered hundreds of FBI agents to the area. He directed sailors stationed in Meridian, Mississippi, to aid in the search. Never before had the federal government helped investigate the disappearance or murder of a civil rights worker. "It is a shame that national concern is aroused only after two white boys are missing," Lewis said. He demanded federal protection for civil rights workers in the future. If further violence erupted, he said, then "blood will be on [the government's] hands."[5]

Meanwhile, with the nation's eyes riveted on

Mississippi, voter registration and Freedom School classes went on throughout the state. Lewis sped from one site to another, sometimes organizing and speaking, sometimes canvassing voters or working with children.

On July 2, with Goodman, Chaney, and Schwerner still missing, President Johnson signed the newly passed Civil Rights Act of 1964. The events in Mississippi had helped to move Congress to make it the law. Now, segregation of public places like restaurants, hotels, libraries, and playgrounds was illegal. Companies could no longer discriminate racially in hiring.

The next day, Lewis gave a speech at a voter registration rally in a Ruleville, Mississippi, church. Across the street lay the ruins of a SNCC worker's firebombed home. In his remarks, Lewis warned his audience not to feel triumphant yet. "The Civil Rights Act is not the end—it is just the beginning. Just as the Interstate Commerce Commission regulations became meaningful only with the bodies of the Freedom Riders, it will still take our bodies and our efforts to make the Civil Rights Act meaningful," he said.[6]

On August 4, six weeks after their disappearance, the bodies of Goodman, Chaney, and Schwerner were finally found buried in an earthen dam at a cattle pond. The black Chaney had been brutally beaten and shot three times. The two white men each died of a single gunshot. The nation grieved deeply along with the victims' families and fellow activists. John Lewis spoke at the funeral of Mickey Schwerner, who had been his friend. Yet the violence did not stop. SNCC documented 450 violent incidents over the three months of the Freedom Summer project, including eighty beatings, thirty-five church burnings, and thirty bombings.

Meanwhile, veterans of the previous year's Freedom Vote in Mississippi organized in preparation for that year's presidential nominating convention. Their plan was to show that members of the state's all-white Democratic Party delegation were not true Democrats at all. Black Mississippi activists who were registered Democrats tried to attend county and state meetings at which delegates to the national convention would be elected. The white Democrats would not even let them in. This violated the national Democratic Party rules for delegate selection. The black Mississippians and their lawyers documented every violation.

Then the black activists held their own county and state meetings, carefully following national procedures. They did not restrict their delegate elections by race; a handful of white Mississippians worked with them. They called their new party, which they believed represented the true Democrats of the state, the Mississippi Freedom Democratic Party (MFDP).

John Lewis crisscrossed the state, giving speeches at county meetings in support of the MFDP. Meanwhile, President Lyndon Johnson nervously kept a close eye on this process. During the summer, Lewis had attended a meeting of civil rights leaders at the White House. He tried to buttonhole the president to persuade him to support the challenge to Mississippi's all-white party delegation. He urged Johnson to agree

From left, John Lewis; Aaron Henry, chairman of the Mississippi Freedom Democrats; Roy Wilkins of the NAACP; and James Farmer of the Congress of Racial Equality (CORE) discuss the challenge to Mississippi's all-white Democratic Party.

to seat the MFDP representatives as delegates to the convention—instead of the "official" delegates. Johnson refused even to discuss it with him. Lewis, undeterred, followed up with a letter to the president. He wrote, "without seating the MFDP . . . the Democratic party and the Federal government can never become the instruments of justice for all citizens that they claim to be."[7]

President Johnson feared that the South, which had voted solidly Democratic for nearly a century, would join the Republican Party instead. In fact, white southern Democrats had already started to do this. Most of the official Mississippi delegates had already announced that they would not vote for their own party's candidate. They would vote for the Republican Barry Goldwater, who opposed the Civil Rights Act. Yet they insisted on attending the Democratic Party's convention to nominate a candidate they did not even want!

Sixty-eight MFDP delegates—sixty-four blacks and four whites—arrived in Atlantic City, New Jersey, in mid-August 1964 for the convention. They had brought along the burned-out shell of the car used by Goodman, Chaney, and Schwerner, as a searing reminder that they were literally risking their lives to attend. Lewis later recalled seeing the MFDP delegates on the Boardwalk, dressed in their best, looking proud and energetic despite having traveled twelve hundred miles by bus from their homes. "It was hard not to be stirred to tears by that sight," he says.[8]

The MFDP delegates planned to meet with the convention's credentials committee. There, they would present evidence showing how they had been excluded from the delegate selection process. They hoped that the committee would disqualify the official delegates and seat the Freedom Democrats instead. When it came time for them to give their testimony, the room was so packed that Lewis had to watch on closed-circuit television from down the hall. Across the country, other Americans watched, too, as part of live convention coverage on television.

The climax of the testimony came from Mississippi native Fannie Lou Hamer. Millions of Americans witnessed her telling the story of how she was fired from her job and evicted from her home for registering to vote; how she was savagely beaten by police after attending a voting rights training course; and how the Freedom Democrats had struggled to get to Atlantic City. She asked "the question we all wanted answered," Lewis said. She asked, "'If the Freedom Democratic Party is not seated now, I question America. Is this America, the land of the free and the home of the brave?'"[9]

So powerful was her testimony that, as she spoke, Democrats nationwide began telephoning their delegates to demand that the MFDP be seated. In the White House, Lyndon Johnson watched, too.

To get Mrs. Hamer off the nation's television screens, Johnson announced that he would hold a news conference to begin immediately. Sure enough, the networks cut away from Mrs. Hamer to show the president.

Johnson knew a formidable opponent when he saw one. A master politician, he began pulling strings behind the scenes with his supporters at the convention. He demanded that the convention offer the Freedom Democrats a deal. They would get two seats, with the promise that in four years, at the next presidential nominating convention, they would not be excluded. Mrs. Hamer's response: "We didn't come all this way for no two seats!"[10]

But the president won this power struggle. The convention voted to accept the compromise even though the Freedom Democrats voted unanimously to reject it. Meanwhile, the Mississippi regulars announced their support for the Republican candidate Barry Goldwater and went home.

"When you play the game and go by the rules," Lewis realized, "you can still lose . . . if you're going to disrupt the natural order of things. . . . We were naive."[11] This was the beginning of the end for SNCC, Lewis later believed. Many black activists stopped trusting any whites after this. Many rejected the political system entirely.

Yes, the price of Freedom Summer had been high. Yet seventeen thousand African-American voters had

Fannie Lou Hamer was determined to let all African Americans know they had the right to vote. "We have never been represented in Washington," she said.

been registered through those efforts. In ten years that number would climb to three hundred thousand. The MFDP challenge had failed, but eighty thousand Mississippians had joined the new party. In ten years, Mississippi would have more African-American elected local officials than any other state in the nation. But this was still to come.

7

BLOODY SUNDAY

In 1964, the Vietnam War was escalating and military service was required for all able-bodied young men. Exceptions had traditionally been made for conscientious objectors—pacifists who felt morally opposed to war. With his commitment to nonviolence, John Lewis was a pacifist. He had applied for conscientious objector status twice and been denied. During the summer of 1964, he appealed to the highest level. The next year, his appeal was granted, making him the first African-American conscientious objector in the history of Alabama.

After Freedom Summer, many SNCC members

collapsed in exhaustion. Lewis now believes that what they suffered was similar to post-traumatic stress syndrome.[1] They had lived as if under siege that summer. Some never recovered.

Entertainer Harry Belafonte, an African American and longtime SNCC supporter, arranged for a group of eleven activists, including Lewis, to spend two weeks in the African country of Guinea. As special guests of the country's president, Sekou Toure, they toured the newly independent nation and met young African activists. Despite all his travels, before this trip Lewis had never seen black airline pilots. Everywhere he went, Lewis said, he was "struck" to see black people "in charge."[2] When the others returned to the United States, Lewis and his roommate, Don Harris, continued to travel through Africa, using money from a small grant they had received. They visited Liberia, Ghana, Zambia, Kenya, Ethiopia, and Egypt. The trip gave Lewis a new perspective on black freedom movements in Africa and the United States. "The struggle is the same," he realized.[3]

Lewis found SNCC in disarray when he returned on November 22, 1964. Projects had been abandoned. No new plans had been made. Money was running low.

Meanwhile, the situation was heating up in Selma, Alabama, where Lewis had been arrested on "Freedom Monday" in 1963. Lewis had continued to visit Selma regularly, even during Freedom Summer. In July 1964,

Lewis was leading a protest at the county courthouse in Selma when the sheriff, Jim Clark, spotted him. Trembling with rage, Clark accused Lewis of being "an outside agitator . . . the lowest form of humanity."

"I may be an agitator," Lewis replied, "but I'm not an outsider. I grew up ninety miles from here . . . and we are going to stay here until these people are allowed to register and vote."[4] Clark promptly arrested Lewis, again.

For several years, SNCC had been helping local activists register Selma's African-American voters, but with little success. The residents grew frustrated with the slow pace and decided to ask Martin Luther King, Jr., and his Southern Christian Leadership Conference (SCLC) to replace SNCC as the community's organizers. Dr. King accepted. Lewis, as a member of the SCLC board, felt loyalty to both groups.

On January 18, 1965, Lewis and Dr. King led four hundred Selma residents to the courthouse. All afternoon, these men and women stood patiently in the freezing cold, waiting to be admitted to register to vote. As had happened so many times before, the registrar was unavailable, supposedly "OUT TO LUNCH" for the entire day.[5]

When the demonstrators had gone home, Dr. King, Lewis, and several others went to Selma's finest hotel, the Hotel Albert. The new Civil Rights Act had made it illegal for hotels to exclude African Americans.

From the time John Lewis was a boy, the Reverend Martin Luther King, Jr., above, was his idol. In the 1960s, Lewis was honored to work alongside civil rights activists like Dr. King and A. Philip Randolph (back).

Dr. King intended to be the first African-American guest at the Albert. As he signed in, a young white man attacked Dr. King, kicking and punching him. Without thinking, Lewis grabbed the attacker and held him until he could be arrested and removed. "That moment pushed me as close as I've ever been to the limits of my nonviolent commitments," he remembered.[6]

Every day SCLC led a new group to the courthouse. The federal government had finally ordered the registrar to open more than two days a month. Some days a few people would be registered, some days none. Blacks in Selma united in protest. One day all the teachers would line up to register, one day the beauticians, and the next day the undertakers. The national media reported on the demonstrations, documenting the white resistance, the mass arrests, and the roughing up of demonstrators.

One day, Lewis took a turn leading the group. Sheriff Clark commanded the demonstrators to line up in an alley at the courthouse back door. Lewis refused. The registrants, he told Clark, "preferred to use . . . the one that black people regarded as the *front* door."[7] Again, Clark arrested him.

Another day, Selma-born African-American attorney J. L. Chestnut emerged from the federal building across the street from the courthouse to see Lewis and the sheriff toe to toe. About twenty registrants waited.

"Turn around and go back," Chestnut heard Clark say. "You are *not* going in."

"The courthouse is a public place," Lewis answered. "We will not be turned around."

Chestnut remembered seeing Clark gripping and twisting his billy club as he spoke. "Did you hear what I said? Turn around and go back," he repeated.

"Did you hear what *I* said? We are *not* going back," Lewis answered.

"This boy is crazy," thought J. L. Chestnut.

Yet a few seconds later, Clark relented. Swearing, he said, "Go on in."

"In that moment," Chestnut said, "I saw that the white South was not invincible."[8]

Still, the pace of change remained achingly slow. As the press televised these daily confrontations, Americans saw denial of the right to vote nakedly displayed. In a news conference, President Johnson said, "All of us should be concerned with the efforts of our fellow Americans to register to vote in Alabama."[9]

On February 18, a young African-American army veteran, Jimmie Lee Jackson, was shot at a voter registration rally in nearby Marion, Alabama. He died a few days later. SCLC announced a march from Selma to the state capital of Montgomery, fifty-four miles away, to protest Jackson's murder.

On Sunday, March 7, late in the afternoon, John Lewis and SCLC's Hosea Williams led nearly six hundred marchers from the Brown Chapel A.M.E. Church to the Edmund Pettus Bridge, which leads out of Selma toward Montgomery. They could not see over the steep span until they reached the middle of the bridge. There at the other side was a "sea of blue," Lewis remembered: "Alabama state troopers."[10] Behind them were row upon row of white civilians deputized that morning by Sheriff Clark, many of them on horseback. Lewis looked down to the muddy water one hundred feet below. "Can you swim?" Hosea Williams asked him.

"No," Lewis answered. Neither could Williams.[11]

The head of the troopers addressed them by bullhorn, commanding them to stop marching and return to the church. He gave them two minutes to comply. Lewis and Williams knelt to pray, passing word back for all the marchers to do the same. Lewis looked at his watch and saw that only one minute passed before the troopers and deputies advanced.

The first trooper to reach him raised his billy club and, without a word, slammed it into the side of Lewis's head. Then he wound up for a second blow. Newspaper photographs caught Lewis lying on his side with one arm raised for protection, the trooper's club high in the air and poised to descend. The second blow fractured Lewis's skull. Dazed, Lewis heard a pop and saw clouds of gray smoke. "Tear gas," he remembered. "It makes you feel like . . . giving up."[12]

With a crushing blow, a burly Alabama state trooper fractured John Lewis's skull during the march from Selma, Alabama.

For the second time in his life, Lewis feared it was the end. "How odd it was to die in your own country so near to where you were born while exercising your constitutional rights," he thought as he slipped into unconsciousness.[13]

The troopers and possemen pursued the marchers across the bridge and through the streets to Brown Chapel, six blocks away, striking them with clubs and whips. Marchers who fell, even women and children, were trampled by the horses. Television and still cameras captured everything. Veteran reporters with years of experience covering the civil rights movement had never seen such police violence perpetrated in broad daylight. The attack has gone down in history as "Bloody Sunday."

When Lewis came to, he staggered back to Brown Chapel. Before the stunned and weeping marchers huddled there, he angrily declared, "I don't see how President Johnson can send troops [all over the world] and can't send troops to Selma, Alabama."[14] As he spoke, he was seeing double.

Lewis's friends took him to the hospital. Admitted with a skull fracture, he spent the night sedated with painkillers. While Lewis slept, Dr. King vowed that the march would proceed. Lewis could not bear to stay out of the action. Two days later, he left the hospital against his doctor's wishes.

When Lewis arrived back at Brown Chapel, he

rounded up reporters and swore to them that the march would not be stopped. A newsman from *Time* magazine watched him in amazement. That young man, with his head so thickly swathed in bandages that it looks like a white football helmet, "is the most indomitable person I have ever met," thought the *Time* reporter.[15]

Alabama governor George Wallace had forbidden the march. SCLC appealed the order in federal court. While waiting for the judge's decision, civil rights activists and angry citizens from all over the country converged on Selma to support the marchers. On Tuesday, March 9, a Unitarian minister from Boston, James Reeb, was attacked and beaten by Selma whites. He died two days later.

This was the last straw for President Johnson. He went before Congress to propose a voting rights bill to carry out the Fifteenth Amendment to the Constitution. The television networks carried his speech live. Lewis watched, along with Dr. King and other leaders, in a Selma home. To his fellow southerners, the president said flatly that it was wrong to deny the vote to any American. "It is all of us who must overcome the crippling legacy of bigotry and injustice," said the president. "And we *shall* overcome." When Johnson echoed the word of the civil rights anthem, Lewis saw Dr. King wipe away a tear.[16] Lewis was moved by the speech himself. He wrote a letter to the president, praising it as "historic, eloquent, and more than inspiring."[17]

The next day, a federal judge ruled that the march could proceed. On Sunday, March 21, more than three thousand people left Selma for Montgomery in a group that would swell to more than twenty-five thousand people from every state at the march's climax five days and fifty-four miles later. National guardsmen,

In response to what he called the "crippling legacy of bigotry and injustice," President Johnson asked for federal troops to guard the civil rights marchers from Selma to Montgomery. "We *shall* overcome," he said.

army troops, and FBI agents, ordered into action by the president, guarded the way. "There was never a march like this one before and there hasn't been one since," Lewis said. "You saw the power of the most powerful country on the face of the earth."[18] Lewis sat on the speaker's platform at the rally outside the state capitol in Montgomery at the march's end. He was honored along with other leaders of the movement, such as Dr. King, Rosa Parks, and A. Philip Randolph. Dr. King spoke and eight Alabama residents presented a petition to Governor Wallace requesting removal of all obstacles to voter registration.

But even then, the bloodshed was not over. That night, a white Detroit housewife named Viola Liuzzo, who had volunteered to drive marchers back to Selma, was murdered on the highway by a Ku Klux Klan sniper. The black teenager in her car escaped with his life by pretending to be dead.

President Johnson signed the Voting Rights Act of 1965 into law on August 6. It ended literacy tests and poll taxes. It ordered the appointment of federal voting registrars in place of bigoted local registrars. The president invited Lewis to attend the ceremonial signing at the White House and gave him one of the pens he used. Lewis remembered the Selma campaign and the passage of the bill as "a high point in modern America, probably the nation's finest hour in terms of civil rights."[19]

8

VOTING RIGHTS ACTIVIST

oday, it seems clear that the events of 1964 and 1965 had broken the back of segregation in the South. In 1966, however, it was not at all clear to many SNCC members. Instead, it seemed that as violence against civil rights activists increased, the situation was getting worse, not better. Many of them began to carry guns and call for armed self-defense. "The road of nonviolence had essentially run out," says Lewis. "It had been Selma that held us together. . . . After that, we just came apart."[1]

Many SNCC members also believed that whites—even white civil rights activists—were not to be trusted.

Lewis always believed that "the civil rights movement must be black-controlled, dominated and led."[2] Yet he also believed that SNCC should model the type of integrated community it dreamed of for society. SNCC's longtime white members were like brothers and sisters to him.

As a pacifist who believed in integration, Lewis had lost his place in the new, more militant SNCC. When the group held its annual conference in May 1966, Stokely Carmichael was elected chairman. Lewis was deeply hurt. "I was married to the movement," he remembered. "It was my whole life."[3] Still, he admitted later, "Part of it . . . was ego."[4]

At first, he stayed loyal to the SNCC organization and its new leaders. Then Carmichael began to use the controversial phrase "black power" in his speeches and statements to the press. Lewis did not like a phrase that frightened people and created a gulf between them. At a Mississippi rally in June 1966, Lewis heard speaker after speaker urge listeners to strike back at the white power structure. When Lewis took the podium to preach nonviolence, the audience walked out. "I felt like an uninvited guest," he remembered.[5] A month later, he resigned from SNCC.

Lewis, age twenty-six, had been a full-time SNCC staffer for three years. He had never earned more than $40 a week with the organization, and he was broke. Fortunately, he received a job offer from the Field

African Americans eagerly lined up to register to vote for the first time. John Lewis said the Voting Rights Act of 1965 was "probably the nation's finest hour in terms of civil rights."

Foundation, a charitable trust that funded civil rights and child welfare programs. The job required him to move to New York City, but Lewis thought it might be good to make a clean break. "I felt lonesome, leaving the movement," he remembered. "I kept thinking 'Where am I going, and why, why?' But I also felt liberated."[6] At $10,000 a year, a good salary in 1966, he would be able to help his family financially for the first time as well.

Change had come to Lewis's home county in Alabama. His parents had recently voted for the first time. Family members could now use the public library. But the schools were still segregated and job discrimination had sent all but one of his brothers north in search of work. His remaining brother in Alabama was a woodcutter living in a rented shack.

Lewis spent a year working and thinking in New York, all the while missing the South. When he received a job offer from the Southern Regional Council to be a community organizer, he gladly moved back to Atlanta. His mission was to help communities establish credit unions, farmers' cooperatives, and other projects in which poor people banded together to help one another economically. Unlike his work at the Field Foundation, "this was hands-on work, and I loved it," he said later.[7]

When Lewis had become chairman of SNCC, he had dropped out of Fisk University in Nashville without completing his bachelor's degree in philosophy. Now that he was back in the South, the university agreed to let him graduate if he took a few final courses and wrote a thesis paper on the impact of the civil rights movement on organized religion in America. "It was something I had been involved in," he said with humorous understatement when he received his degree.[8]

Now that he lived in Atlanta again, Lewis began socializing with old friends. At a New Year's Eve party in 1967, he met someone new. Lillian Miles, a

Californian whose family had southern roots, was a librarian for Atlanta University. She had also worked in Africa for several years.

As a way to see her again, Lewis decided to throw himself a birthday party in February. He bought a new record player and cooked a big batch of his specialty, barbecued chicken wings. Miles thrilled Lewis by showing up in a green minidress covered with peace symbols. "She not only believes in peace, but she wears it on her sleeve," he thought.[9] Later, he found that she had worn the dress only as a fashion statement, not as a political statement, but by then it did not matter.

Lillian Miles was well aware of Lewis's stature in the civil rights movement. She also knew that he was too shy and unassuming to realize his importance. The two began dating regularly. Lewis found her easier to talk to than any woman he had ever known. His friends were amused to hear him express amazement that such a beautiful, intelligent woman could love him.[10]

Lewis also took steps to reconcile with his family. They had had only occasional contact since their shame over his arrests had led his mother to beg him to leave the civil rights movement. His deeply religious parents "more or less think I've lost my way," he said, "but I think they're coming to understand better what I've tried to say and do. We're closer now than in a long time. . . . I have a deep love for them [and] what I consider home."[11]

In 1968, Robert Kennedy, then a senator from New York, ran for the Democratic nomination for president. Lewis had forgiven Kennedy for his initially lukewarm support as attorney general for the Freedom Ride. "There was something so basic, so good and passionate and understanding about him," Lewis believed. "He changed a lot after his brother was killed—he grew."[12] When Lewis volunteered for the campaign, Kennedy snatched him up.

Lewis took a leave of absence from his job and went to work for Kennedy. His first assignment was to register African-American voters and arouse support for Kennedy in the Indiana presidential primary. Lewis had been with the campaign only a few weeks when Martin Luther King, Jr., was assassinated in Memphis, Tennessee on April 4.

Lewis was waiting for Kennedy to arrive at a rally in Indianapolis when he heard the news. "I was numb. Frozen. Stunned," he remembered.[13] Lewis kept his emotions in check during the flight back to Atlanta and during the five days of preparation for the funeral. He remained stoic at the service. Lillian Miles joined him at the graveside ceremonies. Only afterward did he go home alone and open up to his grief. "[King] made me who I am," Lewis believed. "When he was killed I really felt I'd lost a part of myself."[14]

"Where does the Movement go from here?" Lewis asked himself. They still had Robert Kennedy, he decided,

and went back to work.[15] Lewis campaigned for Kennedy in Oregon and California.

On the night of the June 4 California primary, which Robert Kennedy won, Lewis watched the election returns on television in a hotel room with other staffers. They saw Kennedy give his victory speech in the hotel ballroom a few floors below. Then they turned away from the screen to begin the celebration, which Kennedy planned to join minutes later. Suddenly, they heard screams coming from the television. The screen showed chaos in a hallway near the ballroom. Kennedy lay on the hallway floor, shot by an assassin and near death. It had been only two months since Dr. King's murder.

This time grief tore Lewis apart. He fell to his knees, rocking back and forth, sobbing, *"Why? Why? Why?"*[16] He staggered out of the hotel and wandered the streets of Los Angeles in a daze until 3:00 A.M. By then, Robert Kennedy had died. When Lewis flew to Atlanta the next morning, he wept the entire way. "We lost something with the deaths of those two leaders that year . . . that as a nation we will never recover," he believed. "Call it innocence or trust."[17]

Though still wracked with grief, Lewis served as a Georgia delegate to the Democratic National Convention in Chicago in August 1968. Black and white Georgia Democrats mounted a challenge to the official, nearly all-white delegation. They charged that

Georgia practiced the same kind of biased delegate selection that Mississippi had in 1964. This time the challengers and convention reached a compromise. The two delegations split their votes.

Exhausted and emotionally spent, Lewis collapsed when he returned from the convention and had to be hospitalized. Lillian Miles canceled her planned vacation and spent it at his bedside. Lewis realized how much he loved her and asked her to marry him. Later she joked that she had just caught him at a low moment.[18] They were married on December 21, 1968, by Dr. King's father, the Reverend Martin Luther King, Sr.

In 1970, Lewis took over the Southern Regional Council's Voter Education Project (VEP). The mission was to hold voter registration drives and rallies, to conduct citizenship education classes, and to provide transportation to courthouses and polling places. These were all things Lewis had done as chairman of SNCC. But as a sign of the changing times, VEP also did research on African-American political progress and provided services to African-American elected officials.

The Voting Rights Act of 1965 had not changed the South overnight. In some places, blacks were still afraid to register. In other places, powerful whites still exerted illegal pressure to discourage voter registration.

As executive director of the Voter Education Project, Lewis helped create posters in both English and Spanish urging people to register to vote.

One of VEP's tasks was to monitor new state laws that affected voting. In 1971, for example, twenty-three Mississippi counties wiped out all existing voter registrations and forced everyone to re-register. Lewis invited other civil rights leaders, including Dr. King's widow, Coretta Scott King; Fannie Lou Hamer; and one of Georgia's state representatives, Julian Bond, to barnstorm the state with him rallying people to register again. They conducted dozens of meetings. "We must use the vote as a mighty weapon for . . . change," Lewis urged his listeners at one rally. "We [have] a mandate—a mandate from our foreparents, from our fellow citizens and from God Almighty to change the structure of Mississippi and this country."[19]

Time magazine featured Lewis in an article on "living saints" at the end of 1975. It praised him as one of a select company of activists worldwide who had dedicated their lives to love and justice. Naturally, this brought him some teasing from friends and associates. At parties, he saw people pretend to hide their drinks from him and chant, "Here comes the saint" when he appeared.[20]

John and Lillian Lewis, married eight years, had long been trying to have a child. At last they decided to adopt. Through an agency, they found a baby boy, whom they named John-Miles. They brought him home on August 6, 1976, the eleventh anniversary of the Voting Rights Act.

John Lewis

🔲🔲

A few months later, Lewis attended a reunion of SNCC workers held in Atlanta. Lewis was no longer bitter about his break with SNCC. He spent a pleasant evening with his old friends and coworkers, catching up on the changes in their lives. Over and over, they asked him the same question: When are *you* going to run for office?

9

POLITICIAN

n 1972, the South had elected its first African Americans to the U.S. Congress since the turn of the twentieth century. They were Barbara Jordan of Texas and Andrew Young of Georgia. Young was reelected in 1974 and 1976. However, late in 1976, he resigned to become President Jimmy Carter's ambassador to the United Nations.

John Lewis decided to run for the seat Young had vacated, representing Atlanta. "I believe that men and women of good will can and should inject a sense of morality and ethics into the body politic," he said when he announced his candidacy.[1]

The Fifth Congressional District's electorate was 57 percent white and 43 percent black. The popular Young had managed to appeal to voters across racial lines. Understandably, many black Atlantans wished to keep a black congressman in the seat. The election would be a "fusion" race. Twelve candidates, eight black and four white, from both parties, Republican and Democrat, would compete. In order to have the best shot at electing a black congressman, Atlanta's black Democratic leadership would rally around one of them.

The *Atlanta Constitution* reported that the "consensus candidate" would be John Lewis.[2] Coretta Scott King, Martin Luther King, Sr., Julian Bond, and Congressman Young all endorsed him. Yet Lewis denied that he would campaign only for black votes. "I've spent the best years of my life trying to create an interracial democracy," he said. "My record speaks for itself."[3]

Lewis pledged that no one would outwork him in the campaign. He excelled at meeting voters one-on-one, listening carefully to their concerns. However, even after years of public speaking as chairman of SNCC, his speechmaking was still not polished. The *Atlanta Constitution* described his oratory as "wooden." "Style or saintliness?" a political journalist joked. "The transition is not yet complete."[4] Still, Lewis won the newspaper's endorsement over all the other candidates.

Voters went to the polls on March 15, 1977. As it turned out, though, no candidate won 50 percent or more of the vote. A run-off election would be necessary between the two top vote-getters, John Lewis and the white city council president Wyche Fowler.

Both men were liberals, with nearly identical stands on the issues. Both were popular with blacks and with whites. Lewis, who liked and admired his opponent, had campaigned in a gentlemanly manner up to this point. Now he took the offensive. "You see enough lawyers and professional politicians" in Congress, Lewis argued. "I'm on the case of the people."[5] When reporters noted his tougher attack, Lewis quipped, "I tried to do it nonviolently."[6]

On April 5, though, Fowler defeated Lewis in a landslide, 62 percent to 38 percent. The vote split almost along racial lines. Despite the loss, Lewis liked his first taste of running for office. "This is only the beginning," he told his supporters. "We will return."[7] After that race, Lewis knew he wanted to be a congressman someday.[8]

Lewis's father died on Father's Day in June 1977, after having suffered a stroke the previous year. Lewis eulogized his father at a little church near their Pike County, Alabama, home. An enormous crowd turned out for Eddie Lewis's funeral, a sign of how well known and well liked he had been over many years of farming and driving a school bus.

The following month, President Carter nominated John Lewis to be associate director of ACTION, the federal agency that operates volunteer social action programs. Lewis's position would oversee VISTA, sometimes called the domestic Peace Corps, as well as volunteer programs for retired persons. He would direct 125 staff members and more than 235,000 volunteers.

Lewis was well acquainted with the southern poor, but during his two years with ACTION he saw poverty and suffering all over the country. Lewis became more determined than ever to become a policy maker and decision maker in elective office. "I wanted to get on the other side of that table" at congressional hearings, he said.[9]

Lewis resigned from ACTION at the end of 1979. He took two temporary management jobs in Atlanta while he renewed political contacts and decided which elective office to pursue. First he worked for his old employer, the Field Foundation, and then for the National Consumer Cooperative Bank.

Lewis ran for the Atlanta City Council in November 1981 and won a seat with 70 percent of the vote. During his four-year term, he developed a reputation for good service to the people of his district. He met and befriended practically every police officer and firefighter in the city during his term on the council's public safety committee. Both black and white citizens

Lewis, second from left, learned firsthand about conditions in the rural South. Here, he and Julian Bond, right, talk with some field workers.

valued his honesty and fairness. The voters reelected him for a second term in 1985 with a whopping 85 percent margin.

His fellow city council members, however, did not regard him so highly. Lewis frequently criticized them for conflicts of interest, as when one council member sponsored a highway project that would profit his trucking company by a million dollars. Lewis called on all members to reveal their sources of income and made the first disclosure himself. His report showed that he earned only his council salary and a few thousand dollars from consulting fees and speeches.

Lewis "alienated many of his colleagues with a stubborn refusal to engage in practical politics," reported the *Atlanta Journal and Constitution.* Other council members sarcastically called him "the conscience of the council" and viewed him as a humorless nag.[10] Lewis found himself an outcast on the council, unable to get his bills passed.

Congressman Wyche Fowler, Lewis's opponent in 1977, decided to run for the U.S. Senate in 1986. Fowler wanted Lewis to succeed him. But in the intervening nine years, Lewis had made some enemies. If he ran, he would no longer be the favored candidate of Atlanta's African-American Democrats. That honor fell to Julian Bond, Lewis's old friend and fellow SNCC leader, who had become a state senator.

In the early 1980s, the Fifth Congressional District

had been reapportioned as a result of population changes revealed by the 1980 census. No longer did the district have a white majority. Its registered voters now were 58 percent black.

Lewis announced his candidacy in February 1986. At his opening press conference, Lewis immediately took the offensive. "I have never been quoted calling myself lazy," he said, making a jab at Bond, who had once jokingly described himself as "a little lazy."[11] Bond had also been extensively criticized for missing votes in the Georgia State Senate.

Lewis had changed in the nine years since his first congressional campaign. No longer a gentlemanly campaigner, he stayed aggressive throughout the race, disregarding his longtime friendship with Bond. A political reporter analyzed why: Lewis is "a man of fierce determination and competitive drive," he wrote. "He is every inch a politician. His shot at Bond . . . was fully in character."[12]

Of the nine candidates in the field, Bond was the best known and most experienced politician. He took the front-runner's position from the start. All of the Democratic leaders who had endorsed Lewis in 1977 now either endorsed Bond or silently showed that they favored him. But Lewis was undeterred. "People had always underestimated me," he said.[13]

Lewis rose every day before dawn to meet voters heading to work. He continued until well past midnight, shaking hands at discos, theaters, and all-night grocery stores. "John started to win votes by pushing lawn mowers, if the person he visited was cutting grass," a journalist wrote.[14] At community meetings, he repeatedly shared the story of his life, always including his youthful preaching to the family chickens. "Not that *chicken* story again," one opponent was heard to complain.[15] Atlanta's major newspaper endorsed him over Bond and the rest of the field.

In the August 1986 primary election, Julian Bond won the most votes. But his 47 percent total fell short of the required majority. Just as had happened in 1977, a runoff election would be required, this time between Bond and the second-highest vote-getter, John Lewis. The runoff election would be held in only three weeks.

Opinion pollsters predicted that Bond would win handily. Lewis was surprised, therefore, when Bond challenged him to a series of three debates, giving him valuable free citywide television exposure. Lewis had heeded past critics of his speaking ability. He had taken public-speaking lessons and had been coached by a media expert. He made a good showing in the debates and pulled closer to his rival.

A few days before the election, a young boy answered a knock at his family's door. The child looked at the stranger standing there. "It's John Lewis," he called unhesitatingly to his parents. Lewis felt that if

Rising political stars: Andrew Young, right, was one of the first African Americans elected to Congress in the twentieth century. John Lewis, left, and Julian Bond, center—both civil rights activists in the 1960s—ran against each other for the same congressional seat years later.

his face had become this recognizable, the race would be close indeed.[16]

Voters went back to the polls on September 2. Early returns gave Bond the lead, but after midnight the race grew closer. When the final results were tallied at 2:00 A.M., Lewis pulled ahead, winning by only a 4 percent margin. *The New York Times* called it "a stunning upset."[17] "It's almost like a Disney movie," said Bill Campbell, a Lewis supporter who later became mayor of Atlanta. "He was the little engine that could."[18]

John Lewis defeated the Republican candidate Portia Scott by a landslide in the November general election. Lewis and his supporters hired a special railroad car they named the "Freedom Train" to take them to Washington for the swearing in. Lewis was now ready to take his place on the other side of the table.

10

CONGRESSMAN

n January 1987, John Lewis was sworn in as a member of the 100th Congress. Among the newly elected freshmen, Representative Lewis stood out. Veterans in Congress made a point of meeting and greeting him. "This is an authentic American hero," one congressional colleague said of Lewis.[1]

Lewis threw himself into learning the workings of the House and his role as congressman. During his first term, he drew assignments on the interior, public works, and transportation committees. Though these are minor committees, Lewis used his membership on them to benefit his district. Over the years, he would receive credit for improving Atlanta's airport, highways, rapid transit system, and federal offices.

Every weekend he flew back to Georgia to attend community functions and see his family. On "constituent Fridays" Lewis met with anyone from his district who had a problem or wished to speak with him. These grueling days sometimes made him feel "like a doctor who has been seeing patients," he said.[2] Any concerns of Georgians who might have feared that he was too naive or not well spoken enough for Congress "are no longer serious questions," said the head of Atlanta's county government.[3] During his first term in office Lewis was one of only twelve members of the House with a perfect voting record, meaning he had not missed a single vote. Satisfied voters reelected him in 1988 with more than 75 percent of the vote.

At first, Lewis's family expected to move to Washington to live with him. But as the years passed, they decided that staying in Atlanta was for the best. Lillian Lewis felt it was important to keep "a strong presence in Georgia," said her husband.[4] Mrs. Lewis continued to work as a librarian and was promoted to the top administration of Clark-Atlanta University (formerly Atlanta University). In addition, their son, John-Miles, was reluctant to leave his close group of friends and classmates. Lewis's wife and son often spent time in Washington in the summer, and Lewis continued to commute to Atlanta on weekends.

As a congressman, Lewis began receiving honors for his achievements in the civil rights movement. Brundidge, Alabama, where he had attended the Pike County Training School, held a "John Lewis Day" with a parade. Astonished to see the sign for a street named after him, Lewis joked that it made him "look around to see if [I'm] still there."[5]

The training school no longer existed, but not long afterward Lewis attended his two nephews' graduation from integrated Pike County High School. "I just sat here thinking how far we have come," he reflected. The same weekend, Troy State University (formerly Troy State College) held a luncheon in his honor. The school's officials did not realize the role they had played in shaping Lewis's life when they ignored his application to the college in 1958. Perhaps it had been a blessing after all, Lewis said, since it led to his first meeting with the Reverend Martin Luther King, Jr. Things had changed. As officials led Lewis to the head table, they urged, "Sit down. You're a member of the family now."[6]

The same year, Lewis attended the dedication of a civil rights memorial in Montgomery, Alabama. An elderly white man stepped forward and extended his hand. "I'm Floyd Mann," he said. "Congratulations on becoming a congressman."

Lewis thought back to the carnage of the Birmingham bus station during the Freedom Ride of 1961. He pictured the Alabama public safety director who had chased away Lewis's attackers by firing his pistol into the air. "You saved my life," he told Mann. Lewis hesitated for a second, then embraced him. Mann hugged him back.

"I'm right proud of your career," said Mann.[7]

Lewis made headlines in early 1991 as one of a handful of congresspersons opposed to the Gulf War. Still a pacifist, Lewis said, "Negotiation, sanctions, the way of nonviolence . . . must be exhaustively pursued before we even consider the use of weaponry." How did his constituents react to his opposition to this highly popular war? Voters "see me as a very independent person and they think I go with my conscience," he said. Some even explained that "we may never vote for you, but we believe that you've done what you think is right."[8]

It was Lewis's eloquent speech against the war that led House Speaker Thomas Foley to tap Lewis for a House leadership position as one of three deputy Democratic whips. The whips work to count votes and persuade members to vote in support of their party when legislation is presented. This appointment made Lewis the highest-ranking African-American elected official in the country.

Lewis stood with his party to oppose President George H. Bush's nomination of Clarence Thomas to the Supreme Court. Thomas, an African-American conservative opposed to affirmative action, "wants to destroy the bridge that brought him over troubled waters," Lewis said. "[He] is not a role model I want for my son."[9] Yet Thomas (who was eventually approved in the U.S. Senate) noted that the scrupulously fair Lewis had been the only member of the Congressional Black Caucus willing to meet him and discuss his views.

Around this time, Lewis and two other African Americans in Congress met with the governor of Arkansas, Bill Clinton. Lewis became one of the earliest backers of Clinton's bid for the presidency. He pledged "friendship and support to me when only my mother and my wife thought I could be elected," President Clinton said later.[10] In November 1992, when Clinton was elected president, Lewis again won almost three-quarters of the votes cast for his House seat. Soon after, he gained a seat on the powerful Ways and Means Committee, which controls all the money appropriated by the House.

For the first two years of the Clinton presidency, Democrats formed a majority of members of the House of Representatives. But in 1994, Republicans gained a majority for the first time in forty years. The Republicans' winning strategy had been devised by conservative Newt Gingrich, who became Speaker of the House. Gingrich's Georgia district adjoined that of Lewis, and Lewis became the Speaker's archfoe.

"In their own self-described revolution, conservatives

are trying to reshape American politics," Lewis wrote in an *Atlanta Journal and Constitution* editorial. "This revolution, however, strikes many Americans as divisive and punitive."[11] He criticized Republican-sponsored bills that would undercut the school lunch program, the Clean Water Act, and the "motor-voter" law, which allowed citizens to get driver's licenses and register to vote at the same time. When Gingrich and his Republicans struck back at him, Lewis thundered from the House floor, "I will not be silenced."[12] He went on to characterize Republican welfare reform proposals as "angry and mean."[13]

When Gingrich proposed cuts in Medicare—the federal program providing health benefits to the elderly—Lewis again grabbed headlines. He led a group of protesters confronting Gingrich at a conference on Medicare in Atlanta. "Where is Newt? Newt is scared," the demonstrators chanted when Gingrich declined to take the stage in their presence. Lewis, who had also been an invited speaker, should "choose whether to be a Congressman or a demonstrator," Gingrich harrumphed.[14]

But Lewis explained that the protesters needed the drama of confrontation to "educate and sensitize people to the issue." Congressmen do not give up the right to dissent or protest, he believes: "Dr. King used to say, 'The time is always right to protest for what is right.' I believe in that."[15]

In 1995, when Minister Louis Farrakhan announced plans for his Million Man March, Lewis publicly stated that he would not attend. "An all-black march . . . goes against what I have worked for—tolerance, inclusion, integration," he wrote.[16] A cover article in *The New Republic* not long afterward called him the "last integrationist." Lewis denounced those who believe that integration is an old-fashioned or weak concept. On the contrary, he said, "creation of a truly interracial democracy" is the real untried, revolutionary concept.[17] "If I'm the last person in America believing in integration," he has said, "then I will be that person."[18]

In 1998, Lewis published his autobiography, *Walking with the Wind*, to rave reviews. The American Library Association's *Booklist* magazine named it the best nonfiction book of the year. Coauthor Michael D'Orso taped Lewis's memories and traveled with him as he revisited many sites where he had made history during the civil rights movement. When the book appeared, the little library in Troy, Alabama, invited Lewis to speak about his story. Because the library had been segregated during Lewis's childhood, the librarians then took the opportunity to present him with the library card he had longed for as a boy.

Every year Lewis participates in the reenactment of the march across the Edmund Pettus Bridge in Selma, Alabama, in memory of those who gave their lives for voting rights. In 2000, Lewis invited his friend

Congressman John Lewis says he has devoted his life to fighting for "tolerance, inclusion, integration."

President Clinton to lead the march along with Coretta Scott King and himself. At the reenactment, President Clinton said, "I, too, am a son of the South, the old segregated South. Those of you who marched thirty-five years ago set me free too, on Bloody Sunday. Free to know you, to work with you, to love you. I thank you for all that you did."[19]

By 2000, Lewis's seven congressional terms had made him the dean of the state's delegation. No other Georgia senator or representative had served longer in Congress. When Georgia senator Paul Coverdell died suddenly in office, there was talk of appointing Lewis to fill the unexpired term, but it did not happen. Lewis had actually toyed with the idea of running for the Senate against Coverdell in 1997. He has not ruled out an eventual run for the Senate. "It would be a very difficult race, but I think I could win," he has said.[20]

Looking back, said Lewis, "I'm delighted that I decided to run for Congress."[21] He lives modestly in a row house near the Capitol in Washington and still flies to Atlanta most weekends. In his few spare hours he combs flea markets for antiques and rare books about African Americans. His son, John-Miles, graduated from Clark-Atlanta University and works for the Georgia Department of Labor. Lewis calls Lillian, his wife of more than thirty years, "my closest and dearest friend . . . a real soulmate."[22]

When the hotly disputed presidential election of 2000 came down to a recount in Florida, Lewis wrote a blistering editorial for *The New York Times*. Lewis insisted on the necessity of counting all 6 million Florida votes, by hand if need be. "Friends of mine died for this principle . . . of one person, one vote," he reminded a new generation.[23] In January 2001, the Congressional Black Caucus met with the new president, George W. Bush, to discuss the controversial election. "Mr. President," Lewis told him, "we feel very strongly about what happened in Florida because there's some history here . . . people suffered, people struggled, people died for the right to vote." The new president seemed "very moved by these words," Lewis remembered.[24]

Lewis responded to the terrorist attacks in the United States on September 11, 2001, by supporting President Bush. In Congress the next day, Lewis said, "You may destroy our buildings. You may harm and kill our people. But you will never destroy the spirit of freedom and our love for democracy. Our nation is strong and determined. We will never turn back . . . from our commitment to a free and open society . . . at peace with itself. Those who engaged in this madness will be tracked down and will be brought to justice."[25]

Throughout his life, Lewis has pushed forward for what is right, undeterred in the face of violence and hatred. Speaking of John Lewis, his friend President

Clinton once said, "I would pray that somehow America could be infected, every single one of us, with the spirit that has animated John Lewis's life."[26]

"I hear a lot of young people say, 'Oh, if I had been living back then, I would have been involved [in the civil rights movement],'" Lewis has observed. "And I say to the young people, 'You need to find something that is so dear and so necessary that you can be involved in.' . . . I say to young people, 'Pace yourself. Pace yourself for the long haul. Don't be in a hurry. . . . It may take much longer to reach that goal, to create the kind of society we want to create.'"[27]

CHRONOLOGY

1940—John Robert Lewis is born in Dunn's Chapel, Alabama.

1944—Parents Eddie and Willie Mae Lewis buy their own farm.

1957—Enrolls in American Baptist Theological Seminary, Nashville, Tennessee.

1958—Meets Martin Luther King, Jr.; begins studying theory of nonviolence.

1959—Cofounds Nashville Student Movement.

1960—Leads sit-ins at Nashville's whites-only lunch counters.

1961—Is one of the original thirteen Freedom Riders, integrating interstate buses.

1963—Elected chairman of the Student Nonviolent Coordinating Committee (SNCC); gives major speech at the March on Washington.

1964—Leads massive voter registration drive during Mississippi Freedom Summer.

1965—Leads the "Bloody Sunday" march in Selma, Alabama.

1966—Ousted as SNCC chairman by Black Power advocate Stokely Carmichael.

1967—Goes to work for Southern Regional Council; graduates from Fisk University.

1968—Campaigns for Robert Kennedy for president; marries Lillian Miles.

1970—Becomes director of the Voter Education Project.

1975—Is named a "living saint" by *Time* magazine.

1976—John and Lillian Lewis adopt a son, John-Miles.

1977—Runs unsuccessfully for U.S. House of Representatives; appointed deputy director of ACTION by President Jimmy Carter.

1981—Elected to Atlanta City Council.

1986—Wins seat in U.S. House of Representatives.

1991—Appointed chief deputy whip of the House; becomes highest African-American elected official in the United States.

1998—Publishes autobiography, *Walking with the Wind*.

2000—Wins seventh congressional term; becomes dean of the Georgia delegation.

CHAPTER NOTES

Chapter 1. Freedom Rider

1. John Lewis, *Walking with the Wind* (New York: Simon & Schuster, 1998), p. 142.

2. David Halberstam, *The Children* (New York: Fawcett, 1999), p. 256.

3. Taylor Branch, *Parting the Waters* (New York: Simon & Schuster, 1988), p. 395.

4. *Eyes on the Prize*, vol. 2, "Ain't Scared of Your Jails, 1960—1961" (PBS Home Video, 1986) (videorecording).

5. Halberstam, p. 261.

Chapter 2. Sharecroppers' Son

1. Howell Raines, *My Soul Is Rested* (New York: Penguin, 1983), p. 71.

2. David Halberstam, *The Children* (New York: Fawcett, 1999), p. 238.

3. John Egerton, *A Mind to Stay Here* (New York: Macmillan, 1970), p. 53.

4. John Lewis, *Walking with the Wind* (New York: Simon & Schuster, 1998), p. 51.

5. Halberstam, p. 239.

6. Ibid., p. 241.

7. Raines, pp. 72–73.

8. Ibid., p. 73.

9. Ibid.

10. Lewis, p. 58.

11. Ibid., p. 61.

12. Ibid.

13. Raines, p. 97.

14. Lewis, p. 78.

Chapter 3. The Sit-Ins

1. Juan Williams, *Eyes on the Prize* (New York: Viking, 1987), p. 126.

2. John Lewis, *Walking with the Wind* (New York: Simon & Schuster, 1998), p. 84.

3. Taylor Branch, *Parting the Waters* (New York: Simon & Schuster, 1988), p. 264.

4. Lewis, p. 96.

5. Fred Powledge, *Free at Last?* (Boston: Little, Brown, 1991), p. 205.

6. Lewis, p. 101.

7. *Eyes on the Prize*, vol. 2, "Ain't Scared of Your Jails, 1960—1961" (PBS Home Video, 1986) (videorecording).

8. Lewis, p. 103.

9. Seth Cagin, *We Are Not Afraid* (New York: Bantam, 1988), p. 70.

10. Lewis, p. 108.

11. *Eyes on the Prize*, vol. 2.

12. Howard Zinn, *SNCC: The New Abolitionists* (Boston: Beacon Press, 1964), p. 19.

13. Lewis, p. 115.

14. Williams, p. 138.

15. Lewis, p. 116.

16. Taylor Branch, *Parting the Waters* (New York: Simon & Schuster, 1988), p. 394.

17. Lewis, p. 133.

Chapter 4. SNCC

1. John Lewis, *Walking with the Wind* (New York: Simon & Schuster, 1998), p. 144.

2. Ibid., p. 149.

3. David Halberstam, *The Children* (New York: Fawcett, 1999), p. 290.

4. Lewis, p. 151.

5. Ibid., p. 153.

6. Ibid., p. 154.

7. Ibid.

8. *Eyes on the Prize*, vol. 2, "Ain't Scared of Your Jails, 1960—1961" (PBS Home Video, 1986) (videorecording).

9. Lewis, p. 158.

10. Ibid., p. 159.

11. Howard Zinn, *SNCC: The New Abolitionists* (Boston: Beacon Press, 1964), p. 48.

12. Halberstam, p. 312.

13. John Egerton, *A Mind to Stay Here* (New York: Macmillan, 1970), p. 61.

14. Ibid.

15. Lewis, p. 173.

16. Pat Watters, *Down to Now* (New York: Pantheon, 1971), p. 108.

17. Egerton, p. 61.

18. Lewis, p. 185.

19. Mary King, *Freedom Song* (New York: Morrow, 1987), p. 34.

20. Taylor Branch, *Parting the Waters* (New York: Simon & Schuster, 1988), p. 589.

21. King, p. 182.

22. Lewis, p. 200.

23. Ibid., p. 205.

24. Ibid., p. 210.

25. Henry Hampton, *Voices of Freedom* (New York: Bantam, 1990), p. 165.

26. Lewis, p. 220.

27. Ibid., p. 224.

28. Ibid.

29. Cleveland Sellers, *The River of No Return: The Autobiography of a Black Militant and Life and Death of SNCC* (New York: Morrow, 1973), p. 66.

Chapter 5. The Struggle for the Vote

1. Henry Hampton, *Voices of Freedom* (New York: Bantam, 1990), p. 213.

2. John Lewis, *Walking with the Wind* (New York: Simon & Schuster, 1998), p. 238.

3. Ibid., p. 239.

4. David Halberstam, *The Children* (New York: Fawcett, 1998), p. 444.

5. Lewis, p. 240.

6. Claude Sitton, "Negroes Resume Atlanta Sit-Ins After Sidewalk Clash With Klan," *The New York Times*, January 20, 1964, p. 15.

7. Lewis, p. 245.

8. Juan Williams, *Eyes on the Prize* (New York: Viking, 1987), p. 229.

9. Clayborne Carson, *In Struggle* (Cambridge, Mass.: Harvard University Press, 1995), p. 99.

Chapter 6. Freedom Summer

1. John Lewis, *Walking with the Wind* (New York: Simon & Schuster, 1998), p. 266.

2. Ibid., p. 250.

3. Ibid., p. 256.

4. Seth Cagin, *We Are Not Afraid* (New York: Bantam, 1988), p. 344.

5. Clayborne Carson, *In Struggle* (Cambridge, Mass.: Harvard University Press, 1995), p. 115.

6. Mary King, *Freedom Song* (New York: Morrow, 1987), p. 411.

7. Steven F. Lawson, *Black Ballots* (New York: Columbia, 1976), p. 303.

8. Lewis, p. 275.

9. Ibid., p. 279.

10. Carson, p. 126.

11. Ibid., p. 127.

Chapter 7. Bloody Sunday

1. John Lewis, *Walking with the Wind* (New York: Simon & Schuster, 1998), p. 273.

2. Ibid., p. 286.

3. Ibid., p. 290.

4. Ibid., p. 302.

5. Ibid., p. 309.

6. Ibid., p. 310.

7. David Garrow, *Bearing the Cross* (New York: Morrow, 1986), p. 380.

8. J. L. Chestnut, *Black in Selma* (New York: Farrar, Straus and Giroux, 1990), pp. 214–215.

9. Lewis, p. 314.

10. Henry Hampton, *Voices of Freedom* (New York: Bantam, 1990), p. 227.

11. Lewis, p. 326.

12. Howell Raines, *My Soul Is Rested* (New York: Penguin, 1983), p. 212.

13. David Halberstam, *The Children* (New York: Fawcett, 1998), p. 513.

14. Clayborne Carson, *In Struggle* (Cambridge, Mass.: Harvard University Press, 1995), p. 159.

15. Halberstam, p. 514.

16. Lewis, p. 339.

17. Steven Lawson, *Black Ballots* (New York: Columbia University Press, 1976), p. 312.

18. Hampton, p. 237.

19. Lewis, p. 347.

Chapter 8. Voting Rights Activist

1. John Lewis, *Walking with the Wind* (New York: Simon & Schuster, 1998), p. 347.

2. Clayborne Carson, *In Struggle* (Cambridge, Mass.: Harvard University Press, 1995), p. 151.

3. Danny Lyon, *Memories of the Southern Civil Rights Movement* (Chapel Hill, N.C.: University of North Carolina, 1992), p. 175.

4. Paul Good, "Odyssey of a Man—And a Movement," *The New York Times Magazine*, June 25, 1967, p. 47.

5. John Egerton, *A Mind to Stay Here* (New York: Macmillan, 1970), p. 67.

6. Good, p. 47.

7. Lewis, p. 381.

8. "Learning the Hard Way," *The New York Times*, June 7, 1967, p. 40.

9. Lewis, p. 383.

10. David Halberstam, *The Children* (New York: Fawcett, 1998), p. 569.

11. Egerton, p. 69.

12. Ibid., p. 68.

13. Lewis, p. 386.

14. Ibid., p. 393.

15. Halberstam, p. 567.

16. Lewis, p. 395.

17. Ibid., p. 397.

18. Ibid., p. 405.

19. "Sowing the Seeds of Power," *Ebony*, October, 1971, p. 107.

20. Lewis, p. 416.

Chapter 9. Politician

1. David Morrison, "Lewis Enters Race for Young's Seat," *Atlanta Constitution*, December 22, 1976, p. 1A.

2. Ibid., p. 22A.

3. Frederick Allen, "Abernathy in Congress Race," *Atlanta Constitution*, January 6, 1977, p. 6A.

4. Joe Leslie, "3 Emerge as Leaders in Race for Congress," *Atlanta Constitution*, March 13, 1977, p. 6A.

5. David Morrison, "Lewis Rips Fowler, Special Interests," *Atlanta Constitution*, March 22, 1977, p. 1A.

6. Ibid., p. 7A.

7. David Morrison, "Fowler Wins in Landslide Over Lewis in 5th District," *Atlanta Constitution*, April 6, 1977, p. 6A.

8. John Lewis, *Walking with the Wind* (New York: Simon & Schuster, 1998), p. 424.

9. Ibid., p. 428.

10. Frederick Allen, "5th District Contest Pits Bond and Lewis in a Last-Hurrah Effort," *Atlanta Journal and Constitution*, February 9, 1986, p. C1.

11. Ibid.

12. Ibid.

13. Lewis, p. 441.

14. Thomas E. Ball, *Julian Bond vs. John Lewis* (Atlanta: HBCC Publishers, 1988), p. 2.

15. Lewis, p. 444.

16. David Halberstam, *The Children* (New York: Fawcett, 1998), p. 649.

17. Dudley Clendinen, "Ex-Colleague Upsets Julian Bond in Atlanta Congressional Runoff," *The New York Times*, September 3, 1986, p. A16.

18. John Lancaster, "John Lewis' Victory May Well Be Credited to a Lifelong Tenacity: Bald, Bulldog-Built Politician Became 'Little Engine Who Could,'" *Atlanta Journal and Constitution*, September 4, 1986, p. D8.

Chapter 10. Congressman

1. Scott Shepard, "Freshman Lewis Quickly Makes Mark at Capitol," *Atlanta Journal and Constitution*, August 24, 1987, p. A1.

2. Ibid.

3. Ibid.

4. Personal interview with John Lewis, March 26, 2001.

5. Adam Nossiter, "Tiny Ala. Hometown Welcomes Lewis As Hero," *Atlanta Journal and Constitution*, October 4, 1987, p. A19.

6. Tom Baxter, "With Ala. Award, Lewis's Life Comes Full Circle," *Atlanta Journal and Constitution*, June 3, 1989, p. A11.

7. David Halberstam, *The Children* (New York: Fawcett, 1999), p. 651.

8. Personal interview with John Lewis, March 26, 2001.

9. Bob Dart, "Atlanta's Lewis Calls Thomas an Unfit Role Model for Blacks," *Atlanta Journal and Constitution*, September 20, 1991, p. A14.

10. Bill Clinton, "Remarks at a Dinner for Representative John Lewis in Atlanta, Georgia," *Weekly Compilation of Presidential Documents*, March 20, 2000, p. 840.

11. John Lewis, "No Retreat From Past Victories," *Atlanta Journal and Constitution*, March 12, 1995, p. R1.

12. Jeanne Cummings, "Republicans Will Not Silence His Criticism of Gingrich, Lewis Vows," *Atlanta Journal and Constitution*, February 9, 1995, p. A14.

13. John Lewis, "I Spoke Up for the Poor," *Atlanta Journal and Constitution*, May 10, 1995, p. A11.

14. Adam Clymer, "As Demonstrators Gather, Gingrich Delays a Speech: House Colleague Leads Protest on Medicare," *The New York Times*, August 8, 1995, p. B6.

15. Personal interview with John Lewis, March 26, 2001.

16. John Lewis, "Why We Marched in '63," *Newsweek*, October 23, 1995, p. 33.

17. Sean Wilentz, "The Last Integrationist," *The New Republic*, July 1, 1996, p. 22.

18. Annette John-Hall, "The Courage of His Convictions," *Inquirer Magazine*, January 3, 1999, p. 24.

19. "Clinton Leads Group Crossing Edmund Pettus Bridge on Anniversary of Selma March," *Jet*, April 2000, p. 9.

20. Personal interview with John Lewis, March 26, 2001.

21. Ibid.

22. Brian Lamb, "Booknotes Transcript," July 12, 1998, <http://www.booknotes.org/transcripts/50471.htm> (December 4, 2000).

23. John Lewis, "Now We Know That Not All Votes Count," *The New York Times*, December 2, 2000, p. A19.

24. Personal interview with John Lewis, March 26, 2001.

25. "Congressman Lewis Supports Resolution Condemning Attacks on U.S.," <http://www.house.gov/johnlewis/flsmt-attacks.htm> (September 12, 2001).

26. Clinton, p. 840.

27. Personal interview with John Lewis, March 26, 2001.

FURTHER READING

For Middle School Students

Haskins, James. *The Freedom Rides: Journey for Justice*. New York: Hyperion, 1995.

————. *The March on Washington*. New York: HarperCollins, 1993.

Jordan, Denise M. *Julian Bond: Civil Rights Activist and Chairman of the NAACP.* Berkeley Heights, N.J.: Enslow Publishers, Inc., 2001.

Meltzer, Milton. *There Comes a Time: The Struggle for Civil Rights*. New York: Random House, 2001.

Schuman, Michael A. *Martin Luther King, Jr.: Leader for Civil Rights*. Berkeley Heights, N.J.: Enslow Publishers, Inc., 1996.

Walter, Mildred Pitts. *Mississippi Challenge*. New York: Bradbury, 1992.

For High School Students

Branch, Taylor. *Parting the Waters: America During the King Years, 1954–1963*. New York: Simon & Schuster, 1988.

Cagin, Seth and Philip Dray. *We Are Not Afraid: The Story of Goodman, Schwerner, and Chaney and the Civil Rights Campaign for Mississippi*. New York: Bantam, 1988.

Carson, Clayborne. *In Struggle: SNCC and the Black Awakening of the 60s*. Cambridge, Mass.: Harvard University Press, 1995.

Halberstam, David. *The Children*. New York: Random House, 1998.

Lewis, John. *Walking With the Wind: A Memoir of the Movement*. New York: Simon & Schuster, 1998.

Williams, Juan. *Eyes on the Prize: America's Civil Rights Years, 1954–1965*. New York: Viking, 1987.

INTERNET ADDRESSES

John Lewis's Congressional Website
<http://www.house.gov/johnlewis>

Library of Congress, American Memory
<http://memory.loc.gov/ammem/aaohtml/exhibit/
aointro.html>

A History of SNCC
<http://www.ibiblio.org/sncc/>

INDEX

Page numbers for photographs are in **boldface** type.